Water Tales

stories of the coast

by

Belva Ann Prycel

Goose River Press
Waldoboro, Maine

Library of Congress Card Number: 2013906152

ISBN: 978-1-59713-141-4

First Printing, 2013

Published by
Goose River Press
3400 Friendship Road
Waldoboro ME 04572
e-mail: gooseriverpress@roadrunner.com
www.gooseriverpress.com

Cover painting by Belva Ann Prycel.

Acknowledgements...

With special thanks to Roland Barth for his sensitive reading of *Water Tales*, to Guy MacDonald for his enthusiastic response to *"Brigadoon,"* and to my writing group: Kyrill Schabert, Aloisha Pollack, Susan Spinney, Kay Liss, Stephen Jane, and especially Kelly Patton Brook and Joan Grant for their generous encouragement of my work....and of course, to my partner, Lew, who has always been a part of the adventure.

Preface

The following is a collection of short stories and essays gleaned from a lifetime of living, sailing, and painting on the coast. They range from the Delaware Bay and the Atlantic Coast in New Jersey where I grew up, to the shores of the Sheepscot River and the maritime village of Round Pond, Maine. They contain some of the humorous situations, people, and experiences I have encountered along the way.

Like many things in life, my efforts didn't quite take me where I originally intended to go. I began writing what I thought was a serious memoir. I later realized that a few of the stories didn't fit the theme or tone I had set out to achieve in the larger work, so I began to put them aside for another purpose. They ultimately found their common home here, in this collection of water tales.

It is the presence of water that unifies and surrounds all the stories, as it has my life. I hope the reader will enjoy them as much as I enjoyed recalling them.

—Belva Ann Prycel

Up the still glistening beaches
Up the creeks we will hie;
Over the banks of bright seaweed
The ebb-tide leaves dry.

—Matthew Arnold

Bradford's Beach

Every part of the bayshore has a life, a character, a kind of presence that makes it discreetly different from all others. Some Delaware Bay beaches are inaccessible little pockets of gray mud edging the marshy coast; others are silty clay flats at the entrance to tidal creeks; and a few rare ones are short stretches of pure white silica sand that may attract some swimmers, boaters, or bird watchers.

Bradford's was none of these things. It was a feeble block of gravelly, questionable material bordered by a creek with banks of enclosing mud. In May a few horseshoe crabs spawned there, followed by shorebirds devouring the eggs. Hermit and fiddler crabs, herons, gulls and terns sparred and held sway most of the summer season. Nearly inundated at high tide, along the shore only three badly battered fishing cottages peered above the spartina grasses like feckless shipwrecked squatters.

It offered nothing, therefore, and everything. It was my favorite beach.

In the years when I taught painting classes I brought my students to Bradford's, traveling down a potholed gravel road through salthay meadows bordered by sumac, sea lavender, and feathering foxtail reeds. If the day was agreeable, they would cheerily set up their easels and begin painting the rotting wooden rowboats abandoned at the north end of the beach, or perhaps the more ambitious would tackle the drooping shacks and pendulant grasses barely clinging to the shore. For those uninclined to such subject matter there was always the light on the bay, the arc of clouds across the Delaware, or the intimate beauty of sketching a solitary shell cast up by the waves.

If the day was less appealing, or if no wind prevailed, we might be unhappily heralded by mosquitoes or greenhead flies which always caused a retreat to the studio, but usually we were treated kindly by bay winds and rewarded with an interesting bayscape or spectacular afternoon sky. And it was during those early days at Bradford's that I first became enchanted with the luminescent light of the bay.

Those who paint the bayshore know the light is different there. It may be the humidity or the temperature differential between sky and land and sea. Perhaps it's the angle of the sun as the light crosses the bay and dances through the refracting haze.

My friend, Al Nicholson, a landscape painter and passionate bird watcher, always called it the "lambent light." I never knew exactly what he meant by that, but whatever it was, we chased it relentlessly across many a forgotten canvas. As plein air painters, both dedicated and foolish, we persisted despite weather or insects. After all, we reasoned, an occasional fly plastered into the paint gave "an authenticity" to the work; it was, we believed, the "mark of the struggle."

It is also certain that Bradford's was the beach where I learned to love sailing, although the method my husband and I employed was unconventional—and probably laughable.

This was not our fault, for we were poor then, struggling young teachers, and the only boat we could afford was something lost in the annals of boating anomalies called a snark. A tobacco company produced it and advertised their unhealthy product on its sail. Actually, the snark was a styrofoam device, something comparable to a big tapered picnic cooler with a wooden mast stuck in front and a rudder jutting out the rear. When we bought it, or took it off someone's hands, both the mast support and the daggerboard trunk were heavily reinforced with layers of duct tape. Used and battered and pieced and patched in the most cavalier of ways, with two adults and a dog, the snark barely maintained four inches of freeboard, although we reasoned it was styrofoam and, therefore, incapable of sinking.

It was also during the first summer of the snark that we acquired a small feisty Cairn terrier named Arab. He loved water, but hated the snark.

As we plied the bay—me in constant bailing mode with a cut-out Clorox bottle, Lew just trying to keep the sail and rudder roughly working in alignment—Arab busied himself gnawing and worrying his way through the hull, ripping out big chunks of styrofoam. Nothing could deter him from his mission. He was determined, it seemed, to devolve the snark into the padding material of a common shipping crate.

As Arab worked away, we blamed the gouges and teeth marks he left behind on shark attacks. But after the first summer of use, Lew covered the snark with fiberglass and I painted it a powder blue. It was a small improvement, but one which enabled the snark to survive several more summers of Arab's abuse.

I suppose, even after the new fiberglass and the camouflaging coat of color, it was probably clear to all but us that the bay and the snark were rather spectacularly ill-suited to each other. The snark, as you may have discerned, was a trivial pond boat, a lightweight oddity created for gentle lakes and puddles. At Bradford's, the Delaware Bay was a 16-mile wide ocean estuary known for its currents, steep-sided waves, and storms. However, we stupidly, in our insignificant craft, thought the snark could be used on one of the most capricious bays on the eastern seaboard.

After all, we reasoned, it was styrofoam. Unsinkable.

And so, in reckless abandon, we often found ourselves setting sail from Bradford's, and taking a heading due west into the Philadelphia-Wilmington shipping lanes. In this vicinity 10-story tankers pushed walls of water 15 feet high before their capacious bows. Dozens of barges and oceanliners churned like leviathans through the channel, displacing water into towering wakes. In some small measure of humility, I suppose, we never got too close to any of them, though now, in my cautious old age, I shudder to think what could have been our fate had the wind died, or a wake swamped us, or had Arab removed a particularly critical piece of the hull.

This fortunately never happened, but a cautionary incident did occur in our second season behind the duct taped mast. It wasn't a catastrophe, not by any small standard, but we did discover that we were laboring under one rather flagrantly false assumption.

It happened one steamy July afternoon as we were returning from Fortescue, three or four miles downbay from Bradford's. As we slogged along, bailing and sailing, an umber row of storm clouds began gathering darkly across the bay and soon the wind began rachetting up till the previously calm sea became a minor froth of agitated white caps. Gusts strengthened and blew straight out of the direction we needed to go, and although Lew tacked as best he could, the shoreline beside us never changed, the same patch of wind-flattened marsh always remaining irritatingly abreast of the snark. Water began slushing over the bow and I was bailing furiously then with one hand, and holding onto Arab with the other. The Clorox bottle never was put to such hard use. Lew and I both realized it was futile and Lew took a quick detour toward the marsh. Unfortunately as he tacked the boat broadside to a wave we were slapped with a walloping breaker and instantly swamped about 40 feet from shore. It was all fast and yet extraordinarily slow in a dreamlike kind of way: the snark full of water, the Clorox bottle wrenched from my hand, the oars floating, Arab swimming, Lew grabbing the rudder which was drifting off, me clutching the sides of the boat, then suddenly up to my neck in the turbulent bay. It was then that I was shocked, disbelieving really, to feel the unsinkable snark implausibly disappearing beneath my feet. We were adrift. I was uncomprehending. Lost for a moment. And then I heard Lew's voice calling a few watery yards away, "Stand up! Stand up!"

It dawned on me then that I was somehow still standing on the snark, still attached to the object which had fallen far beneath the waves. I stepped off then, almost casually, into muck so deep that I thought if I hadn't drowned already I would be sucked into a marine version of quicksand. Lew somehow made his way over to me, and with some rigorous shaking of the mast, the mud lost its grip and the snark drifted upward, its wet sail shaking and sloshing in the wind. Lew pulled out the mast pole as I awkwardly floundered and sucked my way to shore.

We all dejectedly gathered on the slimy bank, Lew, myself, and Arab, and miserably waited out the storm. Hours later when we snuck home under cover of night, it took vast quantities of water and soap, repeated hosings to remove the last of the caked silt and mud from our bodies, Arab, and the snark. It would take far longer however to restore any old confidence in unsinkability. Never, really.

I guess you could say we were stunningly naive, or simply filled with the invulnerability of youth. It is easy to see that now. But youth has a way of conferring immortality and invincibility on even the most reckless of mortals. And so, this was certainly not the last of our misadventures, nor was it to be the last of the snark's use at Bradford's. For many years we continued to sail from this little beach—though perhaps more prudently thereafter—skimming along the coast to Fortescue, or beaching on the white sands of Gandys, viewing spectacular bay sunsets or catching blue crabs in the silty tributary winding through the marsh.

It was also at Bradford's that I discovered the first amazing remnants of ancient fossilized coral, jewel-like polished sea glass, weathered arrowheads, and all the wondrous cast-off debris that had found its way there.

In the years since, my husband and I have come to own and sail many boats, (vastly larger and better equipped than the humble snark), and have explored much of the Atlantic coast, yet I somehow always felt our days at Bradford's were the best of it.

Occasionally at cocktail parties I am cornered by an inquisitive soul, someone who wants to know about my favorite cruising spots, best remembered sails or ports of call, but I usually stammer and bumble and avoid such queries, for I know that my experiences are not linear, at least not in the ways most people like to recount such things. Nor do I put much stock in "status boats" or high tech gear. I am not concerned about where I am going or how elegantly I can get there...and if I can't hang my feet in the water along the way, then the journey really isn't worth the taking.

I imagine that Bradford's has changed a lot since those youthful days. I don't even know if the road, the beach, or much of anything remains now. It was all eroding very rapidly when we moved north a few years ago. The fishing shacks were gone then, and the road seemed to be quietly disappearing under encroaching vegetation. That is the nature of the bayshore after all. Fleeting. Migratory.

And Bradford's was never anything exceptional really, not even a spot worthy of being named on a map. But when you age, even the simplest places you've known can take on a meaning and an amplitude only recognized with the passing years.

For me, Bradford's was like that. I'll remember it whenever I sail up to a deserted shoreline, jump off the bow of a boat, and sink my feet into the sand of some welcoming little beach. It's still an adventure, still like something I found at Bradford's long ago. And I believe that won't ever change.

Should you find yourself in a chronically leaking boat, energy devoted to changing vessels is likely to be more productive than energy devoted to patching leaks.

—Warren Buffet

Brigadoon

She was a ship built in 1897 and she had all the rust, hogs, patched sails and sistered ribs to prove it. Her name was the *Brigadoon*, and it was a fitting title I suppose, the name of a village and a ship, resurrected only briefly, every hundred years. In point of fact she was a beautiful relic, a survivor from the great age of sailing craft, and though she was crusty and time-worn, she still possessed a certain heritage and a dignity.

It is inconsequential that the timing of her rebirth was not exact, nor need I share with you all the circumstances of her curious renascence, but suffice it to say that at the moment we saw her we were like two dewy-eyed romantics thrust into the suspended time of a mythical Scottish village. We couldn't know it then, but we were about to encounter an experience so anachronistic, so unusual, that even today friends still speak of the *Brigadoon* in a kind of awe.

We lived on a small lake at the time, and our only boating equipment consisted of a battered canoe, and the lowly aforementioned snark. We were both teaching in public schools, but Lew was teaching in a large high school and bringing home what we considered the kingly sum of $6,000 a year. We reasoned with our extra cash flow we could acquire a slightly bigger boat, expand our sailing horizons, travel the coast. We were actually thinking of a modest fiberglass daysailer, but as events would have it, our plans quickly changed.

The ad in the Philadelphia Inquirer read: 45-ft Lawley sloop, built 1897, good as new, $1,500. This was incredible—and amazingly just affordable on our small budget! We plotted and fantasized. Lew had just read Joshua Slocum's "Sailing Alone Around the World," and I had fond memories of my grandfather's oyster schooners and the majesty of old wooden ships. We dreamed of cruising during the summer, living cheaply aboard our expansive floating accommodations. Friends could join us. We might even sail to the islands! This, we thought, was too good to pass up.

Seeing the *Brigadoon* was unnecessary as we had already talked ourselves into buying it before we ever reached the marina on Barnegat Bay. And it was a grand day for seeing such a ship—a stellarly clear fall day with only a few whiffs of steamy clouds from the Oyster Creek nuclear power plant speckling an otherwise flawless sky.

As we pulled into the parking lot of the marina, one elevated object punctuated the scene— an incomparably tall mast, the other vessels arranged like humble serfs around a stately queen.

This imperious one was *Brigadoon,* "our" boat, and I was immediately struck, gobsmacked really, by her intimidating size. Her bowsprit was nearly 6 feet long and jutted halfway across the wharf to which she was restlessly tethered. Her mast was thick as a telephone pole and half again as high. The broadest part of her decks spanned 11 or 12 feet. A score of people could sit on her cabin and still have room to spare.

Running to and from her impressive mast and criss-crossing her 45-foot length, a maze of stays and lines, intertwined coils, wooden cleats and pulleys, lazy jacks and dangling unknown nautical ropery was implausibly festooned. A jib pole and large forward sail lay heavily on the deck, along with boat hooks, anchor, and an old encrusted anchor chain. At the stern, another appendage protruded several feet, something I later learned was called a "boomkin." It visually balanced the bowsprit—and also, (I thought), offered a tentative hope of grabbing onto some last protrusion if cast overboard.

Finally I lay my astonished eyes upon the boom. It was, by any standard, enormous, hewn no doubt from some mighty log felled in a vanquished forest. I considered its girth, the weight of canvas that was sagging it into its weathered cradle, and I guess I instinctively stepped backward, bumping a boat fender lying on the wharf.

The owners must have heard the thump, and the exclamations of wonder emanating from the pier above, for they appeared in the cabin door, two gray heads rising like aging beavers above the impressive felled boom.

"You the folks come to see the boat?" They looked us over, somewhat critically as we clung fiercely to the pier. "You sure got a fine day fer it. Grab that stay there and come on aboard. Mind the deck. She's a little wet now... just washed her down."

We smiled bravely and hefted ourselves across the sizable span of open water from the high dock to the deck below. Then we properly introduced ourselves.

The sellers were called Ed and Fuzz, a couple whom we learned had sailed for decades on Barnegat Bay. Ed had a full red face and veins as big as pencils that bulged on his forearms. He was the color of a cooked lobster, and a jovial sort. Fuzz bore a crown of frizzled brown hair, a pleasant woman who was equally seared and creased by salt and sun.

We engaged in small talk and strode around the decks oohing and aahing as they pointed out *Brigadoon*'s impressive features—the intricate varnished wheel, the brass bell, the curve of her sheer, her trunk cabin, her fine lines.

"She's traditional," Ed said, "nothing fancy equipment-wise in these old wooden ships, but traditional, you know. They don't make 'em like this anymore."

We didn't know a great deal, but we concurred anyway.

She was certainly long and beamy, and she had a rare low freeboard, so we could sail and hang our feet in the bay.

She wasn't modern, that was true, but she was "traditional"—and she had seen some hard use.

Ed had patched and puttied and painted her till the conjugated deposits on her trim and hull looked like the shale layers of an old mining site. Nothing had been gentrified; everything had been nailed, patched, glued down, or painted over.

Ed had applied two metal straps around her hull to strengthen the ribs where a slight sag, called a "hog," had developed. "Most of the old ships have 'em," he said. "She's solid though. Those traditional old boats were made to last. Built in New England she was, and there probably isn't another boat like her on the eastern seaboard."

Again, we agreed.

After a tour on deck we were ushered down a companionway into a dim but well-appointed cabin, with round brass portholes lining the walls. Two wide berths with dark brown cushions added to the gloomy ambience, all separated by a centerboard trunk holding the drop leaves of a long folding table. Behind a panelled bulkhead with a carved seaman's shelf containing rolled maps, was a small galley with a gimbolled one-burner alcohol stove and a sink. On the opposite side forward, sat a requisite and unremarkable head containing the original sink and john. Throughout the cabin, old brass lantern fixtures prevailed, accentuating the antiquity. The engine, however, was less glamorous, a questionable hunk of machinery sunk in the back under the deck, a greasy affair and an area that I gladly left to Lew's inspection.

I vaguely recall that throughout our tour, from somewhere below, occasionally ruminated the sloshing and rumbling of a distant motor—a bilge pump—something Ed assured us was, again, traditional for old wooden boats.

"Those seams just work and swell with use. She pumps out a little after a sail, or when she's first put in the water in the spring. These old ships all take on a little water where they're caulked. She's wood after all."

"Of course," we agreed.

By now we were sitting in the roomy cockpit, sun smiling beneficently on the water, the feel of a great ship under our feet, all that hardware, canvas, and brass—and we were hopelessly smitten.

"Sounds like a fair price," Lew said. "Would you take $200 as a down payment and the rest in a couple of weeks?" We knew we would have to get a bank loan for the purchase, *hoped* we could get a loan at least.

Ed looked a little surprised, probably at the speed of the offer and lack of any nautical dickering.

"Sure," he said slowly, a big smile animating all the sunburned wrinkles of his face. "I think we could do that." And we all smiled and shook hands on it. Fuzz cheerily made some coffee below and we continued to chit-chat, enjoying sitting on the deck, listening to Ed's sailing experiences on Barnegat Bay. In a small conversational pause, as an indirect matter of curiosity, Ed asked, "What kind of boats did you two sail in the past?"

"A snark," Lew replied.

In the silence a few powerboats sputtered by, the bilge pump sucked a few more noisy slurps of water, a laughing gull snickered somewhere overhead.

"You mean you've never sailed anything *bigger*?" Ed asked, eyes getting very large indeed.

We shook our heads.

I recall only that the demeanor in the cockpit abruptly changed to something like a deep paternal sense of concern.

"Well—I think you should take her out—you know—just for a short sail," Ed seemed genuinely helpful, almost frightened. "We can show you the ropes. You get the feel of her. See what she can do? She's a big boat," his eyes shifted to Fuzz who looked deeply distressed..."but really pretty easy to handle," he added quickly.

"Sure," we agreed.

So we were off, Ed pumping and massaging the engine

into groggy life, Fuzz handily casting lines and pushing the unwieldy bowsprit off the dock, then grabbing a stay and agilely jumping aboard as the last piling cleared the beam. We slid backwards then, turning about in the middle of the Forked River, million dollar cruisers and sailing craft densely docked on either side. As we drifted there, on what seemed to me a giant battering ram, Ed pushed the throttle and the *Brigadoon* pointed her great bow to the sea. A delightful wave of cool wind rushed along the hull as we motored out.

We felt like we were riding on a queen as the river slipped by. Soon we passed the last docks and piers on Forked River, then some small resort cottages, and finally rounded a stretch of shivering marsh grass. Ed cleared the channel marker at the mouth of the river where before us the bay stretched ruffled and glittering for dozens of miles. He quickly turned *Brigadoon* into the wind and handed the wheel to Fuzz.

Uncleating a line "Up she goes!" he yelled, pulling like a yeoman, veins bulging in his muscled arms. Shimmying up the colossal mast 700 square feet of canvas clanked and banged and shook the timbers of the hull, rattling and dislodging every unsecured object in the cabin below.

"Fall off the wind! Fall off!" Ed shouted back through the cacophony to Fuzz.

The *Brigadoon* shuddered and shifted like a wakening dinosaur, slowly coming about. Ed crawled back along a handrail and kicked a knob, killing the engine.

In the sudden absence of the motor's drone there was only the percussive batting of the wind against canvas, a high golden triangle billowing out before us, and a boom groaning and shaking, trying to hold a huge breath of air. Then it all grew quiet, and a rush of power reverberated from the keel, through the hull, and up the frighteningly tall mast. It flowed, it seemed, through the very bodies of the riders in the cockpit, and swept us along with a force that drove the bow down into the oncoming waves and spliced the water into sheets of spume careening off the hull.

We were sailing then, flying really, moving effortlessly through the water on a broad reach. Long Beach Island and the Atlantic Ocean lay seductively to the east, and behind us was the whole of the North American continent. There would never be a moment more stirring again. In that instant, I felt, the *Brigadoon* belonged to us.

***

It all took some final working out—the loan, the details, the paperwork—but we managed to persuade the bank officials that we were not insane and posed no major risk to their institution, or ourselves. We claimed official possession of the *Brigadoon* in late October.

Ed and Fuzz even took $100 off the price without our asking. Ed gave us some extra line, and Fuzz included the plastic dishes and a crabpot in the galley. They also left a boathook, some battered fenders, two life vests and some flares. The sailcovers were in bad shape but serviceable. The anchor remained, and the naugahide brown cushions. We were ready. We guessed.

Lew purchased charts of Barnegat Bay and we pored over them at night like two mariners assessing a foreign shore. We knew there were only three or four weekends left till the boat went into winter storage and we wanted to make the most of them.

That first fall sail we mentally planned and practiced and anticipated like two intrepid generals executing a war strategy. The debarkation date was set for a calm day, and on the slack tide to avoid the strong river current. I kept a boathook at the ready and put as many fenders on the hull as we could scrounge up. The old dormant motor choked and sputtered and finally engaged under Lew's insistent prodding. He let it idle docilely, watching it gratefully, while I slipped docklines, holding fast to the last line upwind that linked us to the security of land. As I reluctantly let it go, the bow neatly cleared the end of the dock.

I'm not sure what happened exactly, but I think that *Brigadoon* must have caught a tiny bit of current, or perhaps an errant gust of wind, for her stern began to slip back toward the boat beside us. Lew immediately turned her bow bayward, giving the engine some gas, but then the wicked bowsprit seemed to acquire a life of its own, determined, destined perhaps, to impale an expensive cruiser on our opposite side.

It was on this day that I became intimately acquainted with the prerogative of boat captains to yell mercilessly at their wives. In the midst of screamed invectives I ran forward flailing the boathook and pushed as hard as my 125 pounds would allow off the nearest piling. Our momentum slowed and *Brigadoon* swung sluggishly off again, just barely missing shearing another boat.

Tension-filled and quivering, we sought the center of the narrow river as *Brigadoon* drifted past the marina. I recall a few people came out and waved from the shore like spectators seeing the doomed *Titanic* depart Liverpool. They were curious, no doubt, or maybe wondering how much damage we could inflict with our new purchase. We tried to pass by nonchalantly. Besides, ahead of us the broad waters of Barnegat Bay beckoned.

The wind that day was mercifully light, and we used the lull to practice raising and lowering the main. I went to the wheel, and as I had seen Fuzz do once, I turned the boat up into the wind, keeping my eye on two telltales hanging from a stay. Lew stood by, rope in hand, ready to raise the sail. However the boat over-rotated and I thrust the wheel back in the opposite direction. I suppose I over-compensated again, and we fell off the wind, turning in a series of disorienting circles. It must have been a curious sight had any been watching from shore, seeing the meandering hulk of *Brigadoon* scribing ovals in the bay. After more unsuccessful tries, Lew reached back and revved up the engine. This time the extra power held the ship's nose pointed toward Long Beach Island and he raised the sail.

Brigadoon shook and shimmied then fell off the wind. I breathed a sigh of relief and steered her toward the only object I recognized—the Barnegat Lighthouse, waiting happily for that remembered surge of power that would carry us away. Nothing. There was nothing. We were sitting there. Barely moving. No—leaning over. Actually, we were falling, sliding sideways, literally rolling like a heavy log till the gunnel dipped so far in the water that the cushions fell off the seats and I felt we would capsize—

"What's happening?" I screamed!

"Oh *no*," Lew said, "I forgot to drop the centerboard!" He stumbled below and I heard a clunking of wood and sick screech of metal. In a moment the ship righted and began to move like I presumed a sailboat should move. We were sailing then. At least.

Narrowly surviving the first challenges, we let our racing pulses slow as *Brigadoon* doggedly moved along on an easy tack, ambling gently over an occasional wake from a cruiser or a small ocean swell, heeling only slightly. After a half hour or so, I actually started to relax a little. She was really big, a bit like riding a whale. In fact, everything about her seemed larger than life, even the minor sails and accoutrements like the jib.

Lew tried to raise this strange bit of cloth, testing it in different positions. The extra sail gave *Brigadoon* a jump of speed. After awhile he even ventured to try an unnecessary "reef" in the main, tying all the strange little dangling ropes carefully spaced along the boom. I simply kept my eye on the wind. *Brigadoon* continued to sail along nicely, even under the reef.

I guess I would have been content to go on this way forever, reefed and controlled and coasting comfortably. Unfortunately, the chart indicated shallows ahead—not a big issue with a centerboard—but still who wants to ground a boat on her maiden voyage? So, being prudent we carefully came about, mindful not to jibe the boom. (Actually, the boom was never very far from my thoughts anyway. I was told by Ed that a shift in wind direction from behind could send it instantly careening across the deck, dismasting the ship or dismembering the crew. I always watched it warily. The last thing we needed were head injuries. We'd never be able to pay back the loan.)

So we tacked and looped and made our way across the bay to Long Beach Island, waving proudly to passing yachts, even growing somewhat ebullient, certainly more confident, trying all the different points of sail. I even felt comfortable enough to leave Lew at the helm and to play awhile down in the cabin, organizing the small store of canned goods, maps and clothing we had brought along. Later I made coffee which we sipped on the stern in the fall air, mutually congratulating ourselves on our first sail and our fine boat.

I think it was sometime in mid-afternoon that a gathering breeze off the ocean caught us as we came down the bay. It smelled clean and damp with brine, and soon increased enough to heel the boat more steeply over. It was not a particularly strong wind, not as coastal breezes go, but *Brigadoon* creaked and groaned, strained really, and her mast canted sharply toward Forked River. Quickly she began to take water over the rail. We knew she was "tender" after all, but she was heeling so radically on her side, the huge sail weighing her down, that it gave the sensation of an eminent knockdown. Lew reefed the main again and furled the jib. Still, she didn't sail much better, and now she was moving almost as if she were foundering in a gale, wallowing in the troughs of the waves. She had a wide beam and a shallow draft—not exactly a racing hull—nevertheless her reactions were impossibly sluggish. We wondered, if she sailed this way in a normal breeze, what would she do in really bad weather?

I felt a little ill in all the listing and lolling and went below to visit the head. After taking three steps down the companionway I irrationally felt water coming up to meet me. Floorboards were floating about the cabin, the brown cushions wet and askew, my canned goods sloshing against the berths. What arrested my eye was the oatmeal container. It had sprung open and a coating of gray meally slurry stuck to the centerboard trunk.

"Oh no, we're sinking!" I screamed to Lew. He leaned over the wheel and peered disbelieving into the flooded cabin.

"Geez, her seams must have opened up. Turn her into the wind. I'll drop the sail!"

We quickly got the huge sheet down and I shook uncontrollably as we floundered back to the marina. Lew stayed at the handpump all the way, *Brigadoon* riding low to the water. No longer did the bilge pump thrum reassuringly. The battery was dead. Or swamped. I didn't look below again till we reached the dock. I didn't want to know.

***

"She sink on you yet?" Lil asked.

She was the operator of the Southwinds Riviera Marina, a tough gal who could gut a shark or wither a longshoreman with a glance.

Lew gave her a wan smile and a look that suggested he was deeply engaged in the fishing tackle at the back of the store.

Despite our fitful first sail and the major cleanup involved, I had to admit that all in all, we hadn't done too badly. The bilge pump battery had been recharged and would never again be taken quite so cavalierly; from then on, *Brigadoon* was periodically checked by the marina workers. We had mopped up the mess below decks and Lew did some minor tinkering with the engine which seemed to be running well despite its coating of slime. And we had gotten better at docking and sailing the ship after three more weekends on the bay.

It was the last sail of the season that Guy and Pat MacDonald joined us, a couple just returned from 2 years in the Peace Corps in Nepal and accustomed to a certain level of hardship. Therefore we knew they'd be good sailing companions.

That lovely weekend the trees on the western shore of Barnegat were just beginning to pick up traces of orange and gold as we sailed up the bay to Tom's River. Noisy chevrons of Canada geese passed overhead while Guy lay on the deck, philosophizing, quoting Plato and Seneca. I strummed my guitar at the stern and was making an inept stab at some sea chanties. We puttered all day long, up and down the nearly empty bay, sipping cups of diluted Campbell's clam chowder until the air grew too cool and we turned back in. It was a rare and golden day.

That night, after dinner at a local seafood establishment, Guy and Lew sat in *Brigadoon*'s cockpit smoking Hoya Monterey Cuban Cigars and drinking Malmsey Rare Rich Madeira. Pat and I saw their relaxed silhouettes from the cabin, two figures relishing the lantern light in a gathering darkness. Guy reflectively turned from quoting Plato, to *Lord Jim* and *Moby Dick*. Lew donned a captain's hat, given by my parents, and he wore it with his Scottish wool fisherman's sweater. He looked a fitting captain for *Brigadoon*. Everyone was very mellow, and in this celebratory spirit we toasted the grand ship that had come into our lives.

"To the *Brigadoon*. May she sail another hundred years," quipped Guy.

"Here. Here. To the *Brigadoon*!" we all chimed back.

Brigadoon was headed for winter storage in a few days, but we were nostalgic already, as if we had sailed her for many a year.

The next day Lew and I took down the sails and decommissioned *Brigadoon* for the season. She was one of the last boats to be pulled from the water that fall, and she would be the last to go back in the summer.

***

Snow was fitfully falling. It was early March, but still bitterly cold. We surveyed the interior hull of *Brigadoon*: Lew with a screwdriver poking beams; me holding a feeble light into the cavernous darkness.

"This one's really punky. Pretty bad," he said despondently. "This one here's okay. But...here's another. Not good." So it went, rib by rotten rib.

"Can they be fixed?" I asked.

"I'll have to sister them," came the disembodied voice from the dark. "No wonder she opens up when she sails."

We were to discover this was only a small part of the problem. The transom, essentially the whole end of the boat, was held in place with little more than screws and metal strapping. Rot there had claimed the last rib entirely.

On deck one of the gunnels had cracked and needed to be replaced. The mast had a check, a split, but was probably not in immediate jeopardy, although virtually every part of *Brigadoon*'s surface required stripping, sanding, and varnishing. Now that she was up on the cradle in drydock, we could see that the whole ship should be refastened and every seam recaulked.

I don't know how we did it but we accomplished this all on weekends, beginning that March and extending into late June. It seemed daunting at first, though we were clueless about the degree of effort involved and simply persevered. We learned a lot, by necessity.

Lew engaged his carpentry skills, developed as a teenager when he helped build his parents' house. He made new ribs, screwing them in place while I sanded brightwork. Together we removed the old cotton wadding and recaulked the hull, then stripped the mast and stained and varnished it till it was transfigured into a pinnacle of beauty. The bowsprit and boomkin were taken back to natural wood, as well as the mast hoops and wooden blocks and pulleys. Lew brought the handsome wheel home and refinished it in the basement. We even discovered some intricately carved scrollwork in the bow, and I managed to chisel out the accumulated paint and putty to reveal its amazing detail.

The hardest thing to repair however was the transom. Lew stared at it ruefully, befuddled, for an entire weekend, trying to figure out how to strengthen and stabilize this despairingly rotten portion of the hull. Many came by with opinions: more strapping, stronger screws, extra caulking compound, buy a newer boat. Finally, on a Sunday afternoon as I headed to the marina store to get a sandwich, I saw him standing at the stern, quizzically shaking his head, his tools around him like willing deckhands without a deck.

"Cut it off," I said as I walked away.

I bought a grilled cheese and was standing at the counter exchanging pleasantries with Lil when I heard the distant buzz of a chain saw. When I returned, a gaping hole in the big stern of *Brigadoon* indicated where the transom had once been. She was now officially 44 ½ feet long.

By the end of the spring, after more weekends of unrelenting sanding, scraping, and inhaling paint fumes, we were exhausted. My hands looked like those of a northwoodsman, and Lew and I both had lost fifteen pounds apiece. My parents worried about their artistic daughter—what kind of heartlessly cruel life she had married into. Uncle Bob called this "one worry of a big ship." And we now had taken to referring to *Brigadoon* as "the brig." Had we not been young, I doubt we could have survived her. Still, she was starting to slowly come around, and the product of our efforts was also attracting some admirers at the marina.

Every weekend a few folks would stop by to view the progress of the wreck. Sometimes they would bring coffee or food. We were, I guessed, the crazy young couple restoring the hapless hulk, and we were objects of their general curiosity.

Somehow, we finished up the last work on the exterior as a few people gathered at the dock on the day of her launch. Lew applied the final coat of bottom paint and I put gold highlights in the restored filigree embellishment at her bow. The bilge pump was ready and in fine working form. The mast was ready to step. We proudly affixed a wooden plaque with *Brigadoon* in gold letters off her newly varnished transom. Ed and Fuzz, who had recently purchased a new Alden yacht were there. The Jacksons, the Carnahans, and other dockmates gathered with bottles of wine or champagne to see her off. I had to admit that she looked good.

As the *Brigadoon* slipped into the water and the dockworkers helped us bring her around to her new berth, I stuck a flag in the brass holder at her stern. It was Fourth of July, the height of the summer. And it was truly a rebirth in every way imaginable.

***

The Bay Summer

"Farther to port! A little more...!" I was leaning over the side, hand on a stay, stretched out as far as I could without plummetting into the water.

We were the only boat on Barnegat Bay with enough agility to tack for beer cans, and we assumed this role of unofficial garbage collector and pursued it with diligence and excellence throughout the summer.

"Aha! I got it!" I shouted, the can firmly clutched in my fist, another prize for the trash receptacle.

This sport proved to be just one of many amusements developed on *Brigadoon*, but a rare one available only to those fortunate enough to have a low freeboard. Equally lucky for us, Barnegat boaters were careless or polluting enough to provide us with an inexhaustible supply of beer cans, soda bottles, plastic bags, and styrofoam cups.

It was in this pursuit that we probably developed an ability to gauge not only the wind and tide, but the responses of *Brigadoon* to a fine degree, making us also the only boat able to regularly sail up to our berth, drop sail, and do it all without an engine.

In part, this was a necessary skill, for the engine failed to start much of the time. Nevertheless, we figured that sailors like Slocum had done it, and so could we. No one had engines back then.

Otherwise, when we weren't gathering trash or impressing stunned onlookers with our docking maneuvers, we sailed to Long Beach Island and anchored off a little cove, paddled a canvas raft to the barrier island and walked a quarter mile across blistering sand dunes to the Atlantic Ocean. If there were no stinging jellyfish, the swim was worth it. Or we'd anchor out overnight near the coast, tying up with friends in boats from the marina. Often as we plied the bay, boaters took photos, or shouted comments about the "great old ship." It was gratifying that people knew the *Brigadoon* and appreciated what we had done.

It seemed that many welcome and encouraging companions joined us that first bay summer, including Don Hastings, our landlord and fast friend. He was a handsome middle-aged fellow of Scottish descent—appropriate for *Brigadoon*—single, with a deep thespian voice modulated to equal any Shakespearean actor. Don knew how to relish the moment, tearing up his living room so we could all waltz to tunes around his old player piano. He created fountains and opulent gardens wherever he lived, and molded a life around a love of art, landscaping and antiques. After we bought *Brigadoon* he brought us two 18th century hogscraper candleholders that I proudly used on the ship's centerboard table, (close to the original hog, so to speak).

When Don wasn't antiquing or gardening, he loved to sail, something he discovered that summer on *Brigadoon.*

But while his enthusiasm was a joy writ large, a basic understanding of sailing principles forever eluded his artful brain. More than once we had to rescue him when he upended the snark on Malaga Lake. And on the *Brigadoon*, despite much instruction from us, he was not much better.

If the wind was strong and we were clipping along on a good tack, Don could take the wheel and instantly meander till he lost the point of sail and we sat luffing motionless. At such times he would lament that the wind "always dies when I take over." We didn't have the heart to tell him otherwise. Or he would get so engrossed in a political conversation that he'd nearly jibe the hazardous boom. Sadly, he never learned to gauge wind direction or hold a boat steady by fixing her bow at a point of shore. He was probably near-sighted, but also transcendently careless. When Don was captaining we tacked over crabpots and once nearly rammed the buoy at the mouth of the river. He was a danger to himself and certainly to others. Yet none of this dimmed his prolific enthusiasm. He always assumed his place on the bow at the end of the day, laying on the sprit, hands out on either side, laughing and riding the waves like a portly figurehead.

Our other favorite guests, the hardy MacDonalds, sailed amicably with us, exploring the length of the bay that year. Guy was impulsive and would sometimes jump off the back of the boat without announcement. An excellent swimmer, he could often swim faster than we could sail, particularly if Pat and I took turns being pulled on a raft behind *Brigadoon*. We created quite a drag, but no one cared very much about speed, and it definitely gave Guy a distinct racing advantage.

It seemed too that when not swimming or sailing, we all became acquainted with the life below the bay, catching blue crabs which found their way into Fuzz's crabpot, or clams which made a tasty dinner despite the difficulties of boatside shucking. So it was not unusual that during an oppressively hot summer day we anchored in some shallows and Guy and Lew, feeling with their toes, discerned that the silty bottom was populated by a colony of mollusks. We had wondered what we were going to do for hor d'ouevres that night, but it seemed we now had an answer.

As it turned out these were bay scallops, a rare treat, and Guy and Lew began to collect a few, stuffing them into their bathing trunks. I should note that Lew was a botany major in college, so perhaps he could be forgiven if he was unfamiliar with the locomotion capabilities of certain shellfish. Nevertheless, after acquiring quite a pantsful of these bivalves a strange sort of dance began between the two men, both jumping wildly. I confess I have since only seen rockets or other forms of artillery propelled in such a manner. Soon scallops were being thrown on the deck, heaved with reckless abandon, still snapping as they unceremoniously landed. Guy and Lew quickly scrambled aboard and disappeared into the bowels of the ship.

I can tell you that we ate scallops that night, although Guy now spoke of Plato in a somewhat higher pitch than previously observed. And no one ever scalloped again without a basket or a net in tow.

***

It is sometimes the quests unobtained that retain the greatest power in memory. For us, of all our adventures that summer, the one that stands out the most clearly is the one that didn't happen: the almost forgotten dream of ocean cruising. I think there was a hesitancy, one communicated in the bones and creaking ribs and planks of *Brigadoon*, one we felt in our own bodies each time her aged hull was even mildly stressed. And we knew she had a troubling capacity to take on water, even in a modest blow, so we did not approach taking her to sea confidently. Still—there remained this small unfulfilled desire —and we wondered if we would ever be able to explore beyond the confines of the bay.

It was near the end of summer when Lew checked the

marine radio forecast one morning and announced this was "the day": we would make a try for the ocean. I wasn't sure what exact criteria were met, but agreed anyway. Of course we had been warned that the currents in the inlet were treacherous, even on a slack tide. Still, we viewed it as an adventure worth taking.

It was a clear day, the bay like a sheet of gray silk as we motored south toward Barnegat Inlet, that thin neck of water connecting the bay to the vast Atlantic. Lew had reefed the sail as a backup source of power if the engine failed, and we had life jackets and vests at the ready—even a little tether on Arab. It was an easy approach and *Brigadoon* moved along unperturbed with the outgoing current.

I think we were over a mile from the lighthouse when I could begin to feel the tug of unseen forces converging on the inlet, all the massive volumes of water rushing through a constricted opening to the sea. Billows and moisture began to come in on long swells, those undulations of the deep, voluble and powerful. Soon, waves four or five feet high reared about us and the bowsprit plunged all but under each time it came into the trough of one. In the inlet, lines of advancing breakers fetched up on the shoals for a moment, then fell in cascades of spray. Still we headed out.

The lighthouse steeply loomed on our port side. I was close enough to see tourists on its height and fishermen casting on the beach below. Yet we were isolated from their casual enjoyments, the easy beach life on the shore. I confess that with the nearness of the crowds, so close and yet so distant from us, I felt lonelier than I have ever felt in my life, and immensely vulnerable. We were still only halfway out the inlet but water sucked beneath the hull each time a wave passed, like it was trying to wrench the keel and pull us under. *Brigadoon* shook and groaned. I understood then why Barnegat is considered the most hazardous inlet on the Jersey coast.

I guess both Lew and I felt equally ill at ease. Our engine

was unreliable, and we had little navigating room. We couldn't really depend on sail power here either. Little was said, but while we still had options, Lew sharply swung the boat around. I was relieved when he turned back. We weren't confident the *Brigadoon* could handle it.

Of course it was a disappointment, but really not a major loss. We may not have an oceangoing boat, but we still found Barnegat Bay interesting enough, diverse enough, for our small enjoyments that summer. So we fished, swam, and sailed up into the fall, experiencing halcyon days as well as some bedeviling calms and violent thunderstorms—during which time I ate massive amounts of Sarah Lee pound cake as an anti-anxiety drug. But we could always anchor up a shallow creek and had no real disasters. Then came October.

Few sailing days remained. The weather was changeable, and cool fronts collided with the warmer ocean water out along the coast. Fogs unpredictably wandered in, followed by days of erratic or flukey winds.

Rene and John McGinley, our neighbors at the lake, had been pestering us all summer about sailing on *Brigadoon*, though for some reason we had delayed or simply had other plans. Neither of the McGinleys had ever been on a sailboat before, although both had seen *Brigadoon* once in drydock, and were peskily eager to come aboard.

As our misfortune would have it, the weekend of their visit was a miserable one for a sail of any kind. Shaggy gray clouds scudded over the darkening Forked River, alternately spitting rain. A low pressure system slunk up from the southeast and with it the winds gusted to 20-25 knots. We always avoided sailing in such winds, knowing how poorly *Brigadoon* handled generally, yet the McGinleys were crestfallen.

"Maybe we could just motor out a little way," Rene suggested. She saw a couple of big powerboats depart between squalls and probably couldn't understand why we with our 45 foot ship were so timid. We couldn't tell her that we didn't have twin screws and hundreds of horsepower under our deck, or that the overall wind resistance of *Brigadoon* didn't make for a ship friskily surmounting a gale.

We should have stuck to our guns and stayed in. We should have noticed that no other sailboats had gone out. Probably we felt bad. Maybe we felt guilty because they had driven so far for nothing. I don't know. Whatever our reasons we caved, lost our restraint, and decided to give the McGinleys just a small taste of sail. Lew reefed the main as far as it could furl and we plotted our sail just a short distance out the river. Granted, it wouldn't be much, but it would be the best we could do.

Everyone put on life vests and the McGinleys braced stoically in the cockpit, clutching the seats, backs to the wind. Lew gunned the ship out of the berth, pushing the engine harder than I'd ever seen him do before and we literally shot across the river in reverse, then galloped over our wake and ricocheted toward the bay. The McGinleys hung on for dear life.

We were clipping along like a bus on steroids when Lew raised the castrated sail—still a big wedge of cloth even when reefed—and we heeled over immediately and ran dangerously broadside to the wind. I remember *Brigadoon* made a sound then, one I'd never heard before, a growl almost, her huge lunging hull fighting, driving a furrow through the water, pushing and straining against the crests splitting against her bow. I worried about the Brig, but also about the McGinleys, wet in the back from spray crashing over the cockpit. I thought one or the other would soon be sick, need to use the head, then go below and have a heart attack seeing the floorboards floating. Maybe they would beg to turn around. I hoped that would happen— although when I glanced at them neither bore any indication of pleasure, sickness or distress. And both remained rigidly facing the cabin.

So we plowed past the channel markers, past the last homes where the river opens up at the edge of the bay, past the crab shack where the wind raced through the marsh in a deafening blast. That day it was a disaster—a sudden stormwall of wind, a titanic gust and it pushed the boat over in one devastating roll. *Brigadoon* was knocked down, everything sliding or crashing in the cabin, the mainsheet lying in the river; water rushing over the leeward side of the deck.

I was standing in the companionway when she capsized, and had braced myself against the hatch just in time to see the cockpit shift to a 45 degree angle. I had a brief image of Jon and Rene with their feet pressed against the seats on the opposite side of the boat, and Lew with legs wrapped like a pretzel around the wheel. Very quickly he let go of the sail and *Brigadoon*, which had a weather helm, rounded up into the wind, righting herself, and shaking like a dog, her wet sail luffing and flapping wildly.

I was stunned, dazed as we motored back and said almost nothing. I thought the McGinleys must have been completely traumatized and would never come on a boat again. Even Lew had a slightly green tinge about his eyes.

Then Rene turned to Lew. "Wow, that was FUN!" Do you do that all the time?"

I couldn't believe her words. Both McGinleys were babbling to each other, exhilarated, thinking, I suppose, that sailing was always like this.

"Can we do it again?" Rene asked.

The McGinleys had a bit of verve all right, but for us one knockdown a season was more than enough. It was enough for *Brigadoon*, too.

***

The following week, after the knockdown, the *Brigadoon* went into decommissioning mode, pulled from the water, hibernating on her cradle through the snows. And we went back to work and did few improvements on her that winter.

When she went back into the river in early spring, she

seemed to be taking on even more water than usual, or rather, was in a state that some would consider perpetually sinking. Lew had caulked her again, but it took a long time for her to swell up and tighten. To add to this, the eccentric bilge pump was developing a testy attitude, coughing and sputtering all summer. And then one weekend as we approached the marina, rounding a bend, I realized that I couldn't make out her signature tall mast.

There was *Brigadoon*, sitting on the bottom of the river. A small group had gathered at the wharf to ruminate on her muddy descent. Only the tip of her cabin was visible, decks awash in brown water and seaweed. Lil said they could raise her and not to worry. The pump, or the battery, had obviously failed.

We didn't want to deal with the mess. We had her pulled, and she remained in drydock the rest of the summer. Lew and I cleaned her up inside, removing our soggy clothing, the books, sails and cushions. I washed the wooden walls with mild disinfectant to remove the grease and mold. A few came by and peered inside as I worked, squished their noses and made comments about the smell of dryrot. She clearly needed a complete overhaul and rebuild, the engine was a wreck, and neither Lew nor I had the energy for a total restoration.

Suffice it to say that after a year of storing her at the marina, two young men came along and made a paltry offer. We accepted and the marina handled the transaction. We were a bit sad and nostalgic and on our last visit we removed her nameboard and one brass lantern from the cabin. This was a small part of her that we could retain and remember. I never met the new owners or knew what happened to her after that.

This was all a long time ago, but I still like to think that maybe *Brigadoon*'s sitting, waiting, in some backwater boatyard, that some young couple will come along and see what we saw once, that she'll have another renaissance.

We sailed her for two years and we figured she really didn't owe us anything. I suspect that if she exists now at all, every plank and rib has been replaced in her for a true restoration—the way these things go with old sailing ships where essentially a new boat is constructed around the essence of the old one. The tour guides can then say, "Yes, this 6-inch board here was part of the original chine...and here's a tiny original piece of planking that has all the old stress marks...and oh, this little corner of the companionway to the cabin was saved, and here's the original hatch..." So it goes.

Whatever became of her, she had one rebirth at least, and I always hoped there would be others. It is some small comfort to know that no one we knew ever forgot her, and that is not a bad legacy for a person, or a ship.

We were young and naïve when we saw her, but as Lerner and Loewe once wrote:

"Foolish you may say,
But foolish I will stay...
Brigadoon....Brigadoon,
Where my heart lies:
Brigadoon."

It should be the good fortune of every child
to have at least one crazy uncle."

—John Adams Penn

Uncle Bob

I can't seem to remember a time when he wasn't there. In my earliest childhood I see his loose and gangly appearance accompanied by his inimitable laugh. His name was Bob Henderson. He was my mother's cousin and they grew up together in a tiny tidewater town near the Delaware Bay. That was back in the days when people lived largely off the land or water, growing beans, corn, and sweet tomatoes, or harvesting shellfish from the bay shallows. It was in his youth that Bob first learned his love of the sea, often accompanying my grandfather, Captain Charles Tozour, on the schooner *Warfield* when he dredged for oysters at the mouth of the Maurice River. As my parents had no siblings of their own, he and my mother shared a deep bond of affection for each other throughout their lives. I called him my "Uncle Bob."

It was during the summers of my childhood that I was gifted with seeing Bob everyday. He and his wife, Mary Emma, owned a small beach cottage a short distance from my parents' summer house and it was there that I would happily go to check up on Bobs' latest projects, or more often, to entice him into a game of baseball or horseshoes. In the unencumbered and self-centered logic of children, it never occurred to me that Bob might have more important things to do with his time than listen to the stories of a skinny, preadolescent girl, but such was our relationship that no request was ever deemed too outrageous to be given Bob's serious attention. In fact, the quality I most loved in my uncle was his unfettered spontaneity, an ever-ready playfulness that could be summoned upon any occasion. Unlike the other adults in my experience, he seemed to have retained a childlike enthusiasm and sense of adventure. Anything and everything could divert him from the task at hand.

If the tide was out and the beach sand packed hard and gray to the water's edge, it was "perfect conditions for pitching horseshoes." When Aunt Mary Emma mentioned the words "clam pie," it was a good excuse to scrap chores for clam rakes and traverse the muck of the bay. If the wind direction changed and the sound of breakers carried across the dunes, "Surf's up!" Uncle Bob would yell as he would grab an inflatable raft to ride the glistening waves.

Although incredibly endearing, the consequences of this free and easy attitude were sometimes apparent in the things that were left undone in Bob's life. Even to my child's careless eye, the effects of salt air, sand and moisture were constantly at work on beach dwellings, and Uncle Bob's house was no exception. While he always seemed to have a tool or a paint brush in his hand, his cottage was never completely "together." There were always touch-ups and repairs—the porch trim, the flower boxes, a jammed window here and a squeaky screen door there. Sometimes I would find him under the house tarring pilings, or on the roof examining gutters. I used to call him Mr. Motion. To my mind he was a physical combination of Jimmy Stewart and Red Skelton with a shock of red hair that stood straight in a crew cut and a laugh somewhere between a spasm and a snort. I couldn't pin down his other characteristics because he was never still long enough for closer inspection.

The chairs where he sat—briefly—always had pillows crumpled and askew. While in a seated position he could assume as many contortionist poses as any eastern yogi, sorely testing the structural integrity of any piece of furniture. Today, I suppose, we would call him "hyperactive," but in those days I just thought of him as a rootser.

Uncle Bob worked in the shipyards most of his life, performing a variety of jobs, but primarily he considered himself a caulker. The caulkers pounded cotton wadding between the planks of wooden-hulled vessels. For years I thought that Uncle Bob had something to do with the bottling industry, for he called himself a "corker." But in the South Jersey vernacular, Bob was a "corker" of "ershter boats." And he enjoyed his ershters cooked in their own "lacquer." He also had a decided fondness for "homogized" milk which had recently appeared on the market. But while Bob's fractured pronunciation always elicited howls from my family, he took our laughter in his usual good grace, snorting heartily over bowls of steaming clam chowder or oyster stew served round my mother's claw-foot kitchen table.

Though I'll never forget that most memorable summer when our humor was stretched to its truest limits. That was the summer that Uncle Bob bought the Volkswagon Beetle.

I knew something strange and unprecedented had happened when my father came in the door with a stunned expression and said, "Well, I'll be damned. Bob's out in the driveway in the ugliest car I've ever seen in my life."

This was not a remark I took lightly since my father was a mechanic by trade and knew an ugly car when he saw one—a fact well established forever by my mother and me, learned the year he bought the Rambler Metropolitan. I refused to ride in it except on rare and unavoidable occasions when I would sink down below the level of the windows so none of my friends could see me. So deep was my shame. The whole world then was in love with tail fins, and the Metropolitan had the sexy allure of an inverted bathtub.

Now the Metropolitan had met its equal.

Uncle Bob had the distinction of owning one of the first of this new breed of vehicle whose shape, sound, and inopulent interior we all soon came to know so well. Aunt Mary Emma called it the "Little Volks" and through this name it acquired the status of a kind of family pet.

On hot summer evenings "The Volks" would appear in our driveway, blowing its distinctive gooselike horn—a signal that it was time to make our nightly trek to the custard stand in Strathmere. It was on these nights that I first became aware of the inferior status of women in the world of transport as my father and Uncle Bob would assume leadership positions in the two comfortable front seats, while the three "women" would crowd into the back. My usual place was in the middle, only logical since I was smaller, and a girl, and had shorter legs for straddling the drive shaft.

There I would sit, squashed between the ample hips of my mother and Aunt Mary Emma, directly centered at the vortex of a hurricane. In the laws of air-flow dynamics— in a VW with open front windows—everything whiplashed to the rear, then blew forward. Uncomfortably situated however, we would nevertheless laugh our way to the custard oasis with the weightiest decision of the evening being whether to get a single or a double-dip, chocolate topping or sugar jimmies.

Inevitably, eating this custard in 90 degree weather in such cramped accommodations had its natural hazards. One had to eat quickly to keep one step ahead of disaster. And Uncle Bob, by nature less organized in such matters, was usually too busy laughing to pay much attention to the task at hand and wore more custard home on his shirt or on the upholstery than he ever consumed.

But the sweaty black vinyl seats of the Volks, the texture of a Tyrannosaurus Rex, were unaffected and virtually impervious to stains or spills. Nothing stuck to them except the passengers. Exiting these seats always required peeling oneself away in a slow painful motion, followed by resounding slaps as hot skin and vinyl snapped back into place. Yet despite these logistical problems, the custard stand and Bob's Volkswagon became weekend rituals on summer evenings and we soon grew to accept the vehicle's eccentricities as part of Uncle Bob's own quirky personality.

***

The Volks weathered our good times as well as the usual nor'easters and hurricanes that so often plagued the coast.

I especially recall one October weekend when the seas were enormous as a hurricane centered out in the Atlantic brushed the New Jersey shore. As it passed out to sea, the waves were drawn into frightening mountains of water that crashed onto the beaches, showering piles of seafoam along the dunes and roadways.

I saw Uncle Bob's Volks perched near the top of the dune at the end of our street, positioned against a barrage of suds. He was there, his hands tucked into his pants pockets, clothes flapping wildly and body braced against the elements. I knew his green eyes were looking seaward and could tell by his sniffing dog stance that this was his kind of day.

"Boy, she's kicking up out there," he said as I approached. His excited voice belied that he was relishing the spectacle. "Wouldn't want to be out there in no boat on a day like today. Bet those waves are at least 20 feet high, wouldn't ya say?"

"Yep," I concurred eloquently, so struck was I by the enormity of the scene.

We stood there a long time not talking, just looking at the ocean and feeling the pummeling of the wind and salty foam. As an awkward teenager, I think it was the first time I remember being completely comfortable with a wordless man who wasn't my father.

Later that day, the storm abated and blew itself out somewhere in the cold waters against the coast of Cape Cod. I walked alone with my inflatable raft out to the beach. The sea was eerily calmer now and the wild winds had ceased, but some constrained and furious energy was still churning beneath an otherwise smooth surface. Waves as tall as small houses were rolling against the coast in walls of water—giant, smooth, glass-like funnels of power that built, coiled, and curled in perfect symmetry, crashing upon themselves, then racing in rows to the foam-soaked beach.

I was utterly alone. The broad beach before me seemed to have been swept clean. It was early October but the storm surge that blew up from the south had warmed the sea water to the temperature of tepid bathwater between my toes.

As I stood at the water's edge contemplating my solitude, I heard, faintly, Uncle Bob's laugh. From far up the beach I could barely make out two figures struggling through the surf. Running then as fast as I could, trailing my cumbersome raft, I hurried toward the laughter. Little did I know that among all the days of my childhood, for reasons still unknown to me, this would be the most memorable.

***

I thumped along on the hard-packed sand till the arches of my feet ached. My raft blew behind me, twisting on its coiled rope and constricting my wrist. Sometimes a rogue wave would catch me unawares as a current of water would smash up against my legs and cascade up the beach, forcing me to temporarily alter my course to higher ground. As I ran I passed the remains of the old boardwalk, barnacled pilings that traced a line up the beach and slightly broke the force of the waves, but beyond these, near Uncle Bob's house, the skeletal posts disappeared and I could clearly make out my aunt and uncle between gaps in the giant rollers.

I ran breakneck for the last hundred yards or so, never pausing as I entered the water. Coming up behind Uncle Bob and holding my red raft before me, I inelegantly flopped into an oncoming wave. We were all dragged backwards, Aunt Mary Emma and I squealing with laughter till the wave lost its pull and we could begin anew the task of getting beyond the giant swells.

Oddly, although the breakers were huge that day, they were mysteriously benign and predictable, unlike the choppy dark waters that precede and follow most storms on the coast. There was no wind, no rippling of surface waters, only an uncharacteristic smoothness and clearness to each crest that seemed to have dropped all burden of sediment or debris. Every glowing pale green roller was nearly transparent, rising and curling in astounding uniformity along the length of the beach.

To get beyond the breakers, I would wait until a split second before a wave struck, then toss my raft like a missile over the white water. Grabbing a quick breath I would dive beneath the watery onslaught, emerging beyond the turbulence to move toward the next wall of water, inching out to a point of relative calm.

There, Uncle Bob and Aunt Mary Emma would wait, paddling in circles and eyeing the horizon, lifting and falling over the great swells like weeds on the backs of gentle sea monsters. We were ready to cash in our tickets for the greatest roller coaster ride of our lives. That day there was no need to wait for the perfect watery formation, no difficulty catching the crest of a wave in the precise moment of change as it turns slightly upon itself, no fear of water, or power, nothing but a joy in the moment.

Uncle Bob cheered us on, competed for the longest ride, the biggest wave. He lost control and tumbled into the curls—coming up snorting and laughing and spitting saltwater. He grabbed our toes with screams of "Shark!" He played with the abandon of a five-year-old having a wonderful party.

We rode the great waves that day, sliding off the curls to feel the surge of energy shoving hard at our heels. We flew, nearly popping out of the water as we raced down the glass-like slopes, slamming into troughs, slowing slightly, then gathering speed again to be pummeled and carried to the waiting sand. We laughed, floated and glided all afternoon. We stayed till our stomachs hurt from laughter and our bodies ached with quivering exhaustion, till the saltwater burned our eyes and we could go on no more.

I lay on the beach by the dwindled edge of foam that marked the passage of my last ride. Uncle Bob and Aunt Mary Emma came sliding breathlessly into shore beside me. We were still laughing.

Many years later, Uncle Bob and Aunt Mary were to tell me that this was one of the most amazing days they could ever remember. For me it was too. It was a time of total unselfconsciousness and joy, one of the few times in my life that I have lost myself so completely. I think of Uncle Bob, then, as the eternal child who allowed the child in all of us to be.

As I grew up my summers changed and I saw less of Uncle Bob. I went away to college, married, and soon became absorbed in my own pursuits, but I still saw him at family gatherings and casual dinners on the porch of my parents' home, and during the usual vacations and holidays that mark the passage of our lives. He always could make me laugh, always was ready to tease or tell a joke, and always kept alive the spirit of those days on the coast which we somehow managed to talk about each time we'd see each other. Uncle Bob had the secret for keeping a kind of youthful enthusiasm for living. I never heard him complain about his life, never heard him aspire to acquire more, never heard him question the prospect for the future or the old wounds of the past. He possessed a simplicity for living fully open to the present.

Every child should be blessed with such an uncle as I knew.

Though he has been gone many years, he is still with me in the tides of my life—his playfulness, his enthusiasm, and his joyful love of water. He had no children of his own, but was like a second father to all the children who knew him, and especially to me.

I still keep an inflatable raft hanging by our barn door. You never know when a nor'easter will pass, or a distant hurricane blow up the coast. You never know when the waves may come again. At such times I remember that the gifts of our childhood never leave us—and such a gift was my Uncle Bob.

Portions of "Uncle Bob" were first published in *South Jersey Magazine* in 1993.

Sykes: Come on, snap your fin. Snap it.
You're not snapping it.
Don Lino: I'm snapping it, I'm snapping it!
Sykes: That's okay, a lot of great whites can't do it, yo.

—Sharks Tale

Shark Attack

Lately as I age I have found that one of the commonalities of people who spend time on water is that they are uncommonly fond of recounting their adventures at sea. (Obviously I am one of them.) The more grandiose tales usually involve some element of either joyful exploration or horrific danger—as in the single-handed cruise to Yucatan, viewing Mayan ruins—or some arrestingly dire dismasting in a hurricane. Yet all the stories have some component of surprise, or bravery, or redemption of a briny sort. And so, on such occasions when one-upmanship must prevail, I like to recount the great shark attack off Gandy's Beach.

Gandy's, as you may recall was a frequent destination of the snark, but also the location of the summer house of my longtime friend and artist, Liz Sherman. When Lew and I kept a 23-foot Eagle sloop in Greenwich, New Jersey, we often sailed the few miles downbay to the beach by Liz's house. The shoreline there was blanketed in soft opal-colored sand and it shallowed up gradually so that we could anchor off the beach and easily wade in to Liz and Jim's.

They were a gracious couple who always made us welcome with a glass of wine, a pot of blue crabs, or a bowl of chowder. And always, we would end up on their deck facing westward where the expanse of bay stretched for wave-crested miles to a scalloped wedge of Delaware hills, barely visible above the horizon. Clouds would roll across the water in late afternoon like fleets of grey whales riding on currents that swept from the northwest and held the moisture of the bay crossing in them. We would watch the storms gather and toast the thunder as it boomed and echoed along the shore. By evening, the storms would pass and the atmosphere change, all the haze and heat hanging curtain-like below a disappearing sun, diffusing the light into a hundred subtleties of color. Gold would spectrally shift to orange, then purple, then suddenly everything would glaze over in rose, even the water and the sand of the beach below. The Eagle would sit like a sailing ship in a Turner painting, floating on the water with no line to separate sky or sea.

The last beachcombers and bathers might be heading in, and we would usually go in too, or sail back to the marina in a gentle breeze, seemingly the only vessel on the bay.

Most of our visits passed this way, except for that day on Fourth of July weekend, probably the busiest day that Gandy's ever saw.

Every cottage seemed to have the population of a basketball team, a children's choir, or a class reunion of drinkers and revelers littering its straining decks. I had never seen Gandy's so overflowing or so boisterously loud. Next door to Liz and Jim, the house was rented to a college frat group, and they had started partying three days before the Fourth and showed no signs of relenting. If the troop hadn't wrecked the place manually, or pickled it in alcohol, it seemed they were steadfastly intent on vibrating it down, for the stereo was so loud that it shook the plates in Liz's kitchen and caused the aluminum umbrella pole to tremble like a tuning fork on her deck.

Beyond the celebrating hordes, scores of bathers frolicked and splashed and screamed in the muddy surf. Inner tubes, beach balls, rafts and life rings floated the buoyant throng; dogs furiously chased balls in the water, then shook on the older folks sitting in folding beach chairs, sipping beer. Every now and then a premature firecracker exploded. No one paid attention after awhile. It was, after all, the

Fourth of July.

I was recumbent on a beach towel, hot and sticky and thinking about whether I should try to cool off in the bay. Lew was beside me, placidly reading a magazine, never sweating—a capacity I both envied and resented in him.

I looked past his head, over the bobbing bathers, down the bay toward Fortescue. A couple of powerboats were anchored and people fishing there, fairly far out toward the channel. There was nothing else on the water except a nondescript dark speck, gliding up toward Gandy's, slowly drifting perhaps a hundred and fifty feet off the beach.

Did I say drifting? Was it? And was it really "a speck"? I looked again, holding this thing in my vision until I could see that it was larger than I first thought. In fact, it was pointed, about three feet above the water—a rough estimate—but enough to raise an anticipatory sense of caution around the roots of my hair. I reached over and wordlessly touched Lew's arm, pointing toward the shape, casting a quizzical look in his direction.

"Could that be, maybe, possibly—a shark?"

Lew wasn't sure, but yes, it could be, he said. But still...We sat there quietly watching this black anomaly drawing closer. Then, as such things fortuitously happen, it passed between my line of sight and one of the white powerboats in the distance. At that, my heart stopped. It *was* a shark! And it was heading directly toward the beach.

In the space between the shark and the shore there was a sea of arms, legs, flailing children on kiddy rafts, a boy fishing knee-deep in breakers—and oh, oh no—there was Liz—*swimming out to check her crabtrap!*

I began to scream then, running down the beach, calling out like Roy Scheider in *Jaws*, pointing toward the shark, darkly menacing in the brown waters of the bay. Liz couldn't see it and she couldn't hear me and I panicked. I knew that sharks were here, big ones, all kinds, and the water was unusually warm this year. Already, twice, the beach had been evacuated in Ocean City as a band of sharks were spotted near swimmers. One man had even been bitten. But there Liz was, closer than anyone to this black triangulated power saw, with its thin telltale line of foam behind it, cruising in its unwavering prowl. Sinister. Cold.

I could see in the back of my mind the eye of the shark, indifferent, all instinct-driven, a muscle without pity, its reptilian brain never questioning, never thinking, never expecting compassion nor offering any. I wanted to place a big red X on the water, screaming a warning as in the days of old sailing maps, "*and here there be Dragons.*" But instead I kept up my yelling, "Shark! Shark!"

By now, a wave was rolling down the beach, shouts going from house to house, a rippling domino effect as people came out and lined the deck railings, all looking bayward.

Everyone was out of the water now, except Liz, who was swimming in her relaxed unhurried Australian crawl, nearing the crab trap buoy. I assumed her ears were full of water and she was beyond hearing range.

At this juncture a grey-haired pot bellied man came up behind me with binoculars. "It's a shark all right," he said, handing me an extra pair. "You did a good thing to warn people. My wife and I saw it too and were about to do the same. You never know what's out there."

I squinted in the eyepiece. The shark was huge all right, and deliberately slow-moving, following the current no doubt, right on the surface. Its fin gleamed like polished ebony and the body underneath had to be 12 or 15 feet long with a dorsal fin that big—a real killer, like an iceberg, the greatest menace lurking below in the depths.

In the middle of this horrific imagery I heard the rumble of a motor and realized that Liz's son, John, had shoved their small powerboat into the surf. He was already aboard, gunning the engine and heading out. I watched as this young, bronzed Adonis circled his mother, gesticulating wildly, then he sped maybe another hundred feet in the direction of the shark.

What bravery, I thought. Any fish this big could easily capsize such a small boat, but he had risked his life to warn his mother, had put himself between her and the behemoth of the deep, and she was now quickly swimming back toward shore. I watched, my heart pounding, as he neared the huge fin and I heard John throttle back the engine. He was standing now in the cockpit, a long stake, like a spear, poised over his head. He struck me as a modern Captain Ahab, ready to slay the dragon. But his movements were a bit too cautious, the spear merely a boathook. Perhaps he was going to simply poke the monster, distract it, or maybe too the shark was dead—or better still, a harmless basking shark. But no, he was bringing it aboard! Was he crazy?

The shining thing slid heavily into the boat. John waved and turned toward the beach. I couldn't tell for sure, but I think he was smiling.

Liz had now joined us and the assembled crowd. We all met John expectantly as he coasted the boat ashore. And there, in the bowels of the ship lay the Fourth of July threat, a large, black, ominously bulging plastic bag, full of decaying garbage. It had obviously aged sufficiently to fill with gas, and it was this, one presumed, that had enabled it to float so unerringly, one large point of the inflated bag raising sinisterly above the water.

I was relieved of course, then a bit embarrassed. And I quickly learned that a wise decision has a thousand fathers, but mistakes are forever orphans.

The crowd departed, grunting and shaking their heads as they looked in my direction, some amused, some disgusted at having been diverted from their general carousing; children gleefully returned to the water; Lew walked sheepishly back to the cottage with Liz and Jim. I went back to my beach towel but felt supremely ill at ease after that and soon turned toward Liz's house, almost crashing into one of the frat boys who was staggering up behind me.

He was a little green and glazed over and his breath reeked of beer and something foul seasoned with garlic—a lethal brew whatever it was. He was clearly barely functional and had missed entirely the debacle on the beach.

"Ma'am, you know w-what was, you know, out there? I w-was, you know, out of it for a bit, sssort of half asssleep..." He burped.

"S-someone sssee a sh-shark?" He leered as a bit of spittle drooled off the corner of his mouth. I assumed he had been shipwrecked here for a long time.

"No," I said. "Could have been a shark though. Looked like one but it moved on. Probably just some kind of 'trash fish.' "

"Yeh," he said. He was really more than half gone. "You never know wha-whassout there." He seemed satisfied and lurched away.

I headed up toward Liz's house, never looking back.

If one needs convincing evidence of the capricious nature of the universe, one need look no further than the crab.

—Anonymous

The Claw

I suppose I should have left it there, the claw. I suppose I should have never picked it off the bottom of the tidepool, turned it over, or scraped my fingers along the chitonous serrated pincer. I should certainly never have taken it back to my porch and let it dry in the sun in a spot where I passed it on my way to the garden. It really didn't belong.

First, it was too big, larger than the lobster claws one normally finds at the pounds across the harbor, more massive than the usual tourist fare one got served at the lobster dock. In fact, as claws go, it was gigantic, and although it was cooked, it was not shattered, never cracked by a butter-slathered diner, never deconstructed in the usual way such appendages are eaten.

So it was something of an anomaly, and I unwisely took it home. That was my first mistake.

On the back porch it dried for a good part of the summer, although if it shrunk at all it was in the most undetectable way. The dogs expressed an interest in it for awhile, pausing in their mad rush out the kitchen door as if some olfactory brake had been applied, then relieving themselves and sniffing mightily over the claw remains. But soon, even they became indifferent.

For me, however, it was an uncomfortable reminder, an artifact which activated all the neurons of my aging brain, firing memories of so many disturbing fiddler crab encounters of years past on the Delaware Bay, times when thousands of fiddlers would traverse the marshes in a black wave after a heavy rain, or tie up traffic as they bisected the highway to scale the hills of neighboring farm fields. Always they were waving their huge right claws, and always in a curiously malevolent mood.

The claw has an attitude of open protest that reminds me of all that, fully splayed, likely the last act of an angry lobster before sinking in the roiling stew of the lobster pot, a final gesture of defiance and rage. And why not? For this is surely a horrid way for any creature to die, even one as unsympathetic and morphologically different from us as a lobster. I considered this as I looked across the harbor at the scores of happy tourists, blithely eating away on these strange crustaceans, laughing and amicably enjoying a Maine summer day.

And then I remembered the second mistake, and the unplanned visit to Pemaquid Point on that innocuous August day when we first moved here—the experience that still inspires more than one bad dream and questioning moment. It wasn't expected of course, and it wasn't really wanted, the experience there, but it reminded me that my comfortable little world, and my measurement of it, are severely constricted by a narrow understanding of time. I had been there to Pemaquid, a few times before, watching sunsets and sketching waves, sitting on the rocks with the gulls who always seemed to be facing seaward with me. But on this day, a visit of friends "from away," necessitated that I do more than my usual rock sitting or wave watching. They were sightseers, here to "experience Maine" they said, which I took in their vernacular to mean a lobster for every meal and a visit to all the prime tourist destinations. The latter included not only seeing the lighthouse at Pemaquid, but tediously mulling over all the maritime artifacts in the museum at its base. I confess I had never done this myself, having already seen enough antique lobster traps, tackle blocks, and old photos of Pemaquid to satisfy my curiosity for years. But being a good hostess, I reluctantly went along.

That was the crux of the second mistake. It was, truth be told, not a bad decision at first, for I learned more about lobstering from the cheerful woman who manned the museum than I had expected to encounter. She stood, this petite, gray-haired gentle lady, among the fish spears, giant hooks and grisly entrapments of a bygone fishing industry, with photos of iced in schooners and gutted Atlantic cod, dismasted wrecks and tangled rigging, and recited in the most genteel way the history of lobstering on the coast of Maine. It was a long recitation, but not as long as the time lobstering had been going on here. And in these cold northern waters, depleted of virtually everything else that is edible, these feisty crustaceans were now the dominant species. Survivors.

I considered this as I looked out the lighthouse window at lobster boats coming and going amid miles of buoys, some so dangerously dense on the waters that it was hard to imagine how any boat could navigate here. Yet somehow, as every other fishery had suffered depletion and collapse, the lobster business had been able to continue.

Perhaps this is because lobsters are scavengers and able to eat almost anything disgusting that falls to the bottom, as well as tolerating the extreme conditions of northern winters. They obviously have such a tough carapace that they are unattractive to all but the hardiest of predators, and are only most vulnerable when molting. This leaves them, as lowly bottom dwellers, now virtually the only item on the food chain. But it was not always the case.

In the not very distant past, when other marine life abounded in the north, the lobster was considered a kind of primitive junk food. Native Americans ate them, but generally preferred other fare when they could get it. And in the 1800's, prisoners in the penal system were known to stage revolts over being served too much lobster as a regular food item. Only in the 20th century did the lobster achieve a certain discreet desirability, appearing on restaurant menus and diverse eating venues, and even then it was amazingly cheap to come by. As recently as 30 years ago in Maine, a dollar could get you a lobster dinner with all the accoutrements. Now however, that is no longer possible.

While I'm considering the expense of taking our friends to another lobster feast, our amiable tourguide is continuing her dissertation on lobsters, informing us that the catch will probably be good this year, as new regulations permit only the taking of juvenile lobsters, allowing the youngest to mature and the oldest to remain and reproduce. And it is at about this juncture in her story that I have the unfortunate occasion to look away from the window and toward a corner of the room. It is here, cast in partial shadow, that a yellowed photograph of indeterminate age hangs in sepia drabness. It is of a young girl, 7 or 8 years old, and she is standing before a weathered shed, smiling shyly at the camera. Beside her, nailed to the shed wall, are two objects that stagger the consciousness, the carapaces of two gargantuan lobsters, arms extended on either side, reaching from the ground to over the top of the girl's head.

As if to fully intimidate the viewer and forever seal the fear, beneath the photo in a glass case rests a giant claw, over a foot in width and at least two feet long. I will never look at a lobster in quite the same way again.

***

On idle nights, I sometimes wonder if the tiny land-adapted fiddler crab had achieved the physical stature of the lobster, would those testy throngs have passed me so harmlessly on the marsh roads of long ago? Or if the northern lobsters had banned into socialized armies like the fiddlers, would they so tragically be duped into the confines of the lobster pot? Either way, some things may have worked to our advantage as a predator species on the food chain, and against the crab.

Yet when I think of the claw at Pemaquid Point, and remember the angry fiddlers, I wonder...

I place the claw on the back porch in a bucket with some shells and stones for camouflage and vow to quickly return it to the harbor.

Some debris, along with some thoughts, may best be left at the edge of the tidepool.

"The Claw" was first published in the Goose River Anthology, 2011.

There is nothing that is so aesthetically pleasing and yet so functional and versatile as the canoe."

"Anyone who says they like portaging is either a liar or crazy."

—Bill Mason

The Canoe Down the Maurice

Of all the diverse modes of transportation we have used for getting about on water, the one that has been with us the longest is the canoe. We have used it on lakes, streams, bays, reservoirs, and tidal rivers.

Even when we were engaged in such massive boating debacles as *Brigadoon*, we still kept the canoe. Doubtless this was because, like the snark, it was easy. It was aluminum; you never had to paint it, caulk it, spackle it, sand it, bottom coat or varnish it. As a nearly indestructible form of metal, it could dent but never break. It went over boulders, logs, deadfalls, stone embankments, submerged pilings and sometimes other canoeists without a mark or tear. If it rained, you could turn it over and be dry; if sunny, you could prop it against a rock and be in the shade. It was presentable enough that it created no shame, but common enough that no one would want to steal it. If lost downriver, it could easily be found; if not found, its demise was no great loss. In short, it was a perfect boat.

I can only recall one time, in all the years we used it, that we had a bad experience—and that was our problem and not the boat's—although it stands out in memory as one of the seminal moments in our canoeing experience and certainly contributed greatly to our respect for tidal rivers. Tidal rivers you see, except in their uppermost reaches, are not designed for a canoe.

We should have known this I guess, but we were enraptured in the first days of summer, and succumbed to the need for an adventure. We were yearning for a more challenging outing than the small streams and lakes where we so often plied the canoe. The magnificent Maurice River, a long tidal tributary in southern New Jersey, its source deep in the Pine Barrens and its mouth in the salty Delaware Bay, seemed a perfect prospect. We planned to put our canoe in the river at the city park in Millville and drift on the outgoing current a score of miles past Buckshutem, Port Elizabeth, and Mauricetown. Just a bit further and we could debark at the small boatyard at Matt's Landing. Granted, it was a bit ambitious for a single day, but we were eager, hardy, and wanted to see the river from a different perspective than one gets in rare glimpses from a busy highway. We also wanted to see it more naturally, by paddle or sail, and we snobbishly harbored a fair amount of disdain for the noisy powerboats and "stinkpots" that so often cluttered the waterways.

A chart of the Maurice depicted looping, serpentine meanders in its lower courses, so we estimated that the actual distance traveled, point to point, in river miles should probably be increased by at least a third. Considering this we gave ourselves some extra leeway, leaving early in the morning, a little before the current began running out.

If I said the day was glorious, it would not do it justice, for it was that heartbreaking kind of beauty, the kind found only in early June. At the park in Millville, shaded by ancient trees, the tiny river wandered like a brook in an 18th century pastoral painting, sliding past the crumbling brick arches of the old cotton mills, their windowless walls staring in vine-covered silence—Grecian temples really—with spring grasses and tiny violets breaking through cracks in the mortar. About us, willows and maples hung lushly over the dark embankments. We leisurely paddled along, entranced with it all.

Past the park the sound of traffic broke the reverie as we slid under the High Street Bridge, then behind City Hall and the weed-covered storage yard of a former glass plant. The Industrial Revolution had passed by here long ago, the tall remnant smokestacks standing in the distance, reminders of Millville's manufacturing history. We viewed it all that day from the remove of tangled vegetation and screening deciduous trees, floating by as nature subtly reclaimed the shoreline.

The trip proceeded this way, the noise of commerce dimming, only a few small houses and cabins visible from the river banks. We paddled along on the outskirts of Millville, lazily engaged, till a bit farther south, near Buckshutem, the river gradually began to widen and stretch out impressively before us.

It seemed that each bend brought a new vista, each river mile a wholly different landscape. Sometimes a patch of forest would open up to reveal an early farmstead, a brown sweep of plowed field, or perhaps a bald eagle would fly across the broad bowl of sky to land on a snag by the river. We happily coasted along—voyeurs—barely paddling, moving with the tide, watching the greening banks and the play of life on the river.

It was sometime in early afternoon, in the middle of a wide marsh meadow, when a rare, sandy beach appeared. We took advantage of its accessibility, stopping to eat our lunch. We were ravenous. We ate everything, leaving only some water to sustain us for the remainder of the trip. Unhappily, I was visualizing all the wondrous leftovers back in the refrigerator of our apartment and was perturbed with myself that I hadn't packed more. But there was Lew, the endless proponent of traveling light, and he had dissuaded me. It was, I guess, a practical consideration in a small canoe and I had relented and made just two sandwiches for the day.

We finished our Spartan lunch and I gave a bowl of water and a dog biscuit to Arab, who was already exploring new territory, reveling in the joy of peeing on all the unfamiliar and diverse vegetation. He jumped aboard the canoe, assuming his favorite spot in the bow, and we pushed off again.

"Paddling's gettin' a little tougher," said Lew, looking at the current dragging its burden of dead grass along the side of the boat.

I felt it too, mostly in my upper arms. Resistance. I leaned in and pushed more assertively on my paddle.

But river current wasn't the only issue. It was the wind, just beginning to blow upriver—a really bad omen as we headed toward the big, open, expansive marshes north of Mauricetown.

I guessed we were only about halfway to Matt's Landing, but lacking more inviting alternatives, we simply did what canoeists do: we pressed on, zig-zagging determinedly across the grassy seas of vegetation, the mighty volume of flow of the Maurice now no longer with us.

It was perhaps a couple of hours that we continued this way, and I have to admit there was a great sense of relief when we finally saw the spire of the church in Mauricetown, a citadel on a hill, rising in the distance.

"Not much farther now," said Lew, paddling with new vigor and faux resolve.

I knew he was getting tired, knew he was trying to maintain his prowess at the oars, but I had no such prerogatives.

I simply said, "Great! Can't wait!" my arms and shoulders ached and my lower back was beginning to speak to me in a spasm of pain each time I pressed back on the paddle.

***

It was about then that I reached into the bottom of the canoe to consult the rather useless chart, wondering about the distance we still needed to travel.

"No! Don't stop!" yelled Lew. "You have to paddle or we'll lose ground!"

His voice sounded desperate. I looked at the marsh

beside us. He was right. We were actually slipping backwards. And then I knew it was going to be a longer trip than I thought.

***

Webster's New Collegiate Dictionary defines *meander* as "noted for its winding course, as a stream," or "an aimless wandering, rambling," as "to take a winding or tortuous course, to wander aimlessly..."

This we were doing—rambling, looping, criss-crossing, wandering aimlessly, meandering on the meanders.... The tide turned full and the wind came with it—a major frontal assault in the middle of a vast, open, elemental marsh. Downriver was Matt's Landing, across from the lofty heights of Mauricetown. It was so close, yet so infinitely unattainable....

We had no choice and we paddled without relent, only to circumvent one exhaustingly long meander to discover we were just a few dozen linear feet from where we started. Another hour, another meander, and we came to the dispiriting realization that we had moved laterally less than a couple hundred feet.

The tide was now in a condition that could only properly be described as roaring. To make things worse, the wind slammed us and every muscle screamed in protest.

"Dammit," said Lew, disgusted, "I'm going to carry the canoe!"

Angrily he virtually catapulted out of the boat, unexpectedly sinking in knee-deep mud, the solid looking bank a deceptive illusion: hydric soils—a saturated marine classification of dirt. Muttering through his task, he dragged me in the canoe to the bottom of an overhanging bank.

***

So began the next phase of the trip, something that I can only describe as a grueling and desperately interminable form of *portage*, a muddy drag through muck and grass and assorted vegetative debris to the next twisted meander. There we would make a slippery descent down a mudbank of fiddler crabs, all testy and offended, to re-enter the canoe like mud-caked fugitives, paddle across the next roiled stretch of water, then agonizingly repeat the process.

I was irate then. But neither of us had much energy for complaint. We were too exhausted. And besides, now the temperature was dropping and our feet and bodies were wet and caked in mud.

At about this time I discovered that sandals are an entirely inappropriate footwear for traversing a marsh. On one particularly difficult portage I tripped and slammed my big toe into a raft of dried foxtail reeds and felt something hard and knifelike jam under my toenail. I screamed in pain.

For those unfamiliar with the marsh, the foxtail reed, or phragmites, is known for its sturdy towering height and tassled plumes, but was once also used as roofing material by early colonists. Its stalks dry almost as hard as wood and it splinters into sharp longitudinal fragments when broken. It was just such a fragment that found its way into my big toe. The pain was reminiscent of a Chinese torture—shoving bamboo sticks under the fingernails of prisoners.

I sobbed, dropping the canoe.

A few well placed adjectives gathered loudly then around a four-letter word. I didn't care. No one could hear us anyway. We might as well have been in the peaks of the Himalayas or some Amazonian rainforest. Mauricetown still sat cathedral-like on a distant hill, and Matt's Landing was as remote as the surface of a dim galaxy.

Besides, we were filthy and bleeding—frightening sights—and at that point would have been grateful for a ride—no—*undyingly indebted* for a ride—grateful beyond all possible parameters of normal gratitude—but only one big powerboat came by. The oblivious driver didn't even glance in our direction. Worse, he nearly swamped us in his inconsiderate wake. At that moment I figured we were back in the 18th century in a kind of metal dugout; and he, with his giant cavitating engine, was well-situated in the 20th. I began to curse the canoe.

Lew anchored us with his paddle onto a mudbank and we sat in place against the fierce current till our muscles stopped screaming. Then off we went again—paddling and portaging, portaging and paddling—seeing Matt's Landing appearing and disappearing behind a seemingly limitless sea of reeds like a mirage that shimmers and fades before the eyes of the hopeless. Time became irrelevant then, insubstantial. We were simply locked in an interminable effort, doing what we had to do, existing in some detached zone of grungy despair.

I don't remember when the wind stopped. It was sometime before dark when everything stills on the river. I do know it was getting late because the sun was hanging low, and the glare cut sharply across the bow of the boat. We only had the current to deal with then, and even that was diminishing. For a brief time, I had the sense we might be over the worst, that maybe a meal of hot food, some tweezers, antiseptic, a hot bath and a comfortable chair were in the not-too-remote offing.

Then I heard a slap, followed by "Oh, damn!"

The mosquitoes had arrived.

***

A few years ago I was told that a scientist from Rutgers conducted a study of mosquitoes in all parts of the state. This was apparently done in an effort to determine why some areas have such high incidences of encephalitis and other insect-borne maladies, relative to the mosquito population. The unfortunate results of this research revealed that

Mauricetown had the highest percentage of mosquitoes per square foot of any place in New Jersey. I was never completely clear on the qualifying rationale—whether this was square foot of air, square foot of river, or square foot of marsh. Whatever...it would have been a sobering piece of information had I known it back then. Unfortunately I only knew that the air whined in biting black clouds, and that our ratio of speed, to boat length, to paddle thrust, to current, made us a virtual sitting meal.

I guess that amazing reserves of strength can be summoned in the midst of immense despair—like an Olympic runner who has reached a point of quivering exhaustion yet manages to pull it together for one last grueling lap—or a mountain climber who scales the last hundred feet of sheer cliff in an astounding demonstration of physical resolve.

Anyway, that's what we both did then. It wasn't discussed, wasn't acknowledged. There was no plan, no final "row one for the Gipper," and no question about the necessity of the act. We simply pushed, jamming the paddles like our lives depended on it.

The mosquitoes spurred us on in their perverse way, their density and proclivity for sucking blood as motivating a factor as any I've ever encountered.

Somehow, over an exhausting and indeterminate period of time, the boat ramp at Matt's Landing materialized.

I don't know how to qualify our response then except to say that an almost mystical sense of relief enveloped us as we reached the shore, nearly driving a furrow with the canoe up the parking lot.

We saw our car, the magnificent old black Corvair— the fender-dented, mud-spattered, salt-rusted, one-eyed, cigarette-stained miracle of modern technology—and we staggered toward it. Arab immediately jumped onto his little bed on the back seat; I fumbled in my bag for a Kleenex to wipe blood from my face. Outside, swarms of mosquitoes were hurling themselves against the windows, but inside we sank into the coffee stained seats in a kind of elegant rapture.

When we got home that evening I remember feeling an intense gratitude and pleasure in everything—the hot water, the bath, the soft bed, the food in the pantry, Bengay.....

And I know that we never took an ambitious canoe trip again. Not ever. Our paddles were henceforth confined to lakes and streams, and always reserved for a few easy hours of paddling at most. We never considered taking the canoe on a large tidal river again.

We still have the canoe and it is still a great boat. We have it leaning against the side of the shed here in Maine. Thirty years of use have not affected nor diminished it in the least.

Some friends who like to canoe recently suggested we take it down the Sheepscot, over the Reversing Falls, past Wiscasset, toward the bay.

I told them we had done that once, on another tidal river, and besides, we have a stinkpot now.

If you feel the urge, don't be afraid to
go on a wild goose chase.
What do you think wild geese are for anyway?"

—Will Rogers

A Goose Story

I think it was when we moved to Sheepscot that I first became aware of birds. I am not a bird watcher, so this was a new experience for me, but I could not observe them in a peripheral or casual manner, not as a desultory observer, for they insinuated themselves too intimately in the everyday life of the river, and into my own life by degrees.

In the first winter, after I began feeding the gulls, a few always stood watch on my porch roof , surveying me through the kitchen window, waiting to see if the bowl of scraps on my counter might somehow involve them. The rest of the flock congregated on the frozen marsh at the base of our hill, alert for a movement of the screen door, or a figure passing at the back window, or even, as I later discovered, for some unknown communication of *intention.*

This puzzled me, for they were never fed in a scheduled way, yet they uncannily seemed to know when I thought about committing the act, rising up in unison and flying to the yard where they would patiently wait, turning away from the kitchen window in a kind of avian nonchalance. This phenomenon always left me wondering what else they knew, what communication ability they had which I lacked.

But it was when ice flows blocked the river and covered the mudbanks, when snows piled thigh-deep on the ground, when other forms of sustenance were denied them, that their presence became a wintry background persistence. It was then that our crumbs and table scraps—and moistened kibble which we bought in 50-lb. bags at the market—became their primary sustenance.

I gradually assumed this provider role the first few winters we lived here, but it was on the fifth winter that I became acutely aware of geese.

Of course the river knew many flocks of them, always passing through, the Canada geese and other migrants, but it was the domestic geese that caught my attention. At least a dozen were usually out on the river, or sometimes on the roadway leading to the sheep farm. They were not particularly appreciated by residents, especially since they had rather pesky temperaments and could elongate their necks and come squawking and wagging their tongues and aggressively going after summer walkers. My neighbor was afraid of them and refused to walk near the road where they often gathered. Others, of a conservation mindset, thought they were an annoyance that fouled the waters with their prodigious droppings. In general, you could say they were not liked.

I had mostly ignored them and erroneously assumed that they were owned by the sheep farm people, perhaps because I had seen the woman who lived there throw bread to them in winter. But I soon discovered that I was wrong; the flock belonged to no one. I was also about to encounter an experience so strange that I doubt I will ever fully understand it. Years later I am left with only the words of my mother, who when confronted with anything the least mysterious or unexplainable would say, "I guess that's just the way of it."

For me particularly, "the way of it" happened one cold January morning as I stood in the yard, throwing bread and kibble to the flock of gulls. A heavy snow had come in the night, and with it a brutally frigid wind blew in from the north. The snow was deep and I stomped a little flat space with my boots where I could more easily feed the birds when I sensed a larger figure present at my feet. I looked down, perplexed, to see a goose, hungrily and fearlessly devouring the bread, seeming perfectly at home with the flock of gulls who dined with him.

As I tossed slices into the yard, he leaned in close to me, nearly standing on my boots, with his mouth open as if demanding that I feed him more, or first.

Frankly I was stunned, for the geese in my experience had always been wary or unfriendly with people, and had certainly never separated from the larger flock. For them, predators were always a fear, and they instinctively banded together for protection, or so I assumed. But this goose had clearly very different ideas.

I looked out on the frozen river and the icy, steep hill leading up to my yard, and wondered if he was so hungry that he had come by this unlikely route. The other way, the road over the Sheepscot Bridge, was not as snow-covered but had a fairly heavy burden of traffic, and no geese had ever been known to cross it. Or had they?

I did recall seeing a goose, about a week before, standing in the middle of the bridge next to a stopped car. The driver had gotten out, tucked the uncooperative goose under his arm, and walked back to the Grange where I observed he placed him near the river. I had never seen anything like this before, but hadn't, until this moment, given it much thought. Perhaps this was the same goose, and perhaps he had been on his way to my yard when he was intercepted by the motorist?

Whatever the circumstances, after a good feeding that day, the gulls left, but the goose remained.

***

I'm not sure where he stayed those first cold days. It may have been under some shrubbery against the side of the house where a carpet of evergreen needles made a kind of bed. I doubt he ever crossed the river again, for each day when I fed the gulls, he would suddenly be there. Insistent.

And it was about that time that he began to devolve from an insistent visitor to a nuisance.

It seemed that no longer was the shrubbery, or the bread, a sufficient engagement with the people who lived here. Now he started to show an interest in the porch, so much so that we assumed he was trying to move in.

We watched as the newly winterized porch screens with their covering of plastic, filled with gaps and pokes and goose holes. He was on the back step then, everyday, working away at making an entrance, and nothing could deter him.

We tried shooing him off, but that had no effect. Then Lew put plywood over the accessible parts of the porch, but our intruder was determined and still remained on the step, poking at the wood, squawking and being an annoyance.

In puzzlement and some desperation, I resurrected the poodle carrier as a goose den, putting it on the top step and filling it with straw, then covering it with an old blanket when I put our visitor inside at night.

In this mode of accommodation, he seemed perfectly happy to remain for a week or so, and the desperate pecking ceased. Gradually, the two of us developed a little routine. I would get up in the morning and take him out of the den, remove the soiled straw, put out clean, unfrozen water, then give him bread and poultry pellets. It was also about this time, as we were getting a bit more intimate, that I noticed the peculiarity of his left foot.

It was an odd color, the outer wedge going from a bright orange to a sort a pasty yellow. I remembered that the foot had been slightly discolored since he came here, but in the past few days he had developed a pronounced limp.

I searched the internet for information on geese, trying to find out what this could be.

After coming up empty, I decided to call our vet.

"Is the goose wild?" she asked.

"No, he's a domestic goose, but he lives wild on the river, I think."

"What kind of domestic goose is he?"

"I don't know—a brown one."

"Is he yours?"

"No, not really. I'm not sure where he belongs. I heard the flock was abandoned on the river years ago."

"I'm really sorry, but we don't treat birds."

The conversations all went pretty much this way as I neared the depressing bottom of the yellow pages under "veterinarian." Then, a friend fortuitously suggested I call a new vet in the area, one not even listed yet, who treated farm animals. Maybe she could look at the goose.

***

The next morning our visitor, whom we now unoriginally called Mr. Quack, was *not* removed from his poodle crate. The two dogs watched intently as we loaded a noisy bird in the back of the van and headed off to Wiscasset. I can say that our avian friend was more than a little annoyed at this inconvenience. As we reached the vet's office, I, too, was dismayed to see the carrier, which was clean when we left, covered in a generous splattering of goose droppings. Lew and I scrabbled around for some old newspapers in the back of the van and changed the dirty ones under the carrier.

It had been a long morning already. We were tired, having made our first trip to the vet, only to be told that we needed to go to the wildlife center at Chewonki where a biologist was required by state law to examine the goose. He had to be officially declared a domestic breed before he could be treated. I was never clear on the reasoning for all this, only aware that such bureaucracy meant a longer circuit of Wiscasset at a time when an unhappy goose desperately wanted to be out of the crate.

But we were at our destination at last, sitting in the office with a dirty goose positioned between a dachshund and a German shepherd. We were, ourselves, crumpled and goose-stained and not smelling very good. In such moments, one deeply appreciates a touch of human kindness, and at last we encountered that with Dr. Dowdy.

She was a cheerful woman, just starting a new practice, and she carefully examined Mr. Quack's foot while I held him in a towel. It didn't look like frostbite, she said, or any disease process, rather it seemed some form of trauma.

"Could his foot have been run over by a car?" she asked as she felt the webbing and the odd discolored tissue around the nail.

"I don't know," I replied, but then I remembered the car on the bridge, and recalled the other vehicles that flew along Dyer Neck Road where the flock sometimes wandered. "I guess it's possible," I corrected myself. "We live near a highway and I do see geese along the road sometimes."

"Well, it's good you brought him in," she said, "for this skin is necrotic, dead, and should be removed." She made a semi-circle with her finger, scribing a large portion of the outer web.

"Can you operate on it? What are his chances?" Lew asked, getting right to the heart of the matter.

"I don't know for sure—-I want to check with an avian expert down in Massachusetts first. I've never operated on a bird before."

"But you think you might be willing to try?" I asked hopefully.

"I think so. Leave him here, and if I can get an answer, I'll call you today." Then, seeing my face fall..."Don't worry," she said. "We'll take good care of him. He'll be behind the desk right here in the office, away from the barking dogs. He'll be fine."

True to her word, Dr. Dowdy got the requisite information and operated the next morning, and in the afternoon Mr. Quack returned to where he'd always longed to be: the porch. He arrived somewhat chastened and quiet, with a bandaged foot tied in several feet of surgical gauze, and we acquired an even longer list of instructions.

To begin, he needed antibiotics twice a day, ¼ of a pain pill every few hours, clean straw, much fresh water, and most difficult of all, his bandage needed to be changed with clean salve and dressings applied every day. This would necessitate two people, one to hold and one to treat. It seemed rather daunting. Neither of us had ever really handled an injured goose before. We were friendly with him of course, but not chummy in the way one would be with a dog or a cat. Geese are not naturally inclined that way.

I wondered how this was going to work—and Lew was more than a little annoyed at being dragged into another animal rescue. But as I looked at the forlorn creature in the poodle crate, I felt determined that we had to try.

"He came to us, to *me*, and I just can't ignore that. He's here now." I said.

And before long, indeed he was, homesteading on the porch, or rather, assisted living on the porch.

***

The Rehab

From the beginning it was obvious the crate would not be suitable for an extended stay, and I have described that our porch was enclosed in plastic, but cold in February. I worried about this unduly—a minor issue I later learned since geese have heavy coats of down and are acclimated to cold quite well. Rather it was the goose droppings that proved a bigger problem. They were more abundant than I could imagine. This we ultimately solved by putting plastic tarps on the floor, then covering them with straw. The straw needed to be shoveled out every few days as our formerly pleasant porch became a kind of pungent holding pen. I was glad, however, that geese never achieved the stature of goats, or I would not have been able to keep up the pace, for I discovered that food and water make rapid fire passage through the alimentary canals of geese like road runoff through a storm drain.

Gratefully, it was sometime during these first few days of medicating and shoveling and feeding and bandaging that Lew introduced some organization into the mayhem. He made a little portable sort of corral, a wooden goose fence for a section of the porch. This enabled us to confine our friend to a smaller area while the rest of the space piled up in goose pellets, water bowls, bales of straw and bandaging supplies.

Generally, Mr. Quack was cooperative in all things, even as we mucked around trying to work this out. He ate well, took his medicine in bread, and quietly bedded down at night. The only thing he truly disliked was the bandaging, and this proved problematic, especially trying to keep the wound clean and dry. Sometimes we would change the dressing twice a day, particularly if Quack had been pecking at the gauze or managed to soil it completely—which was most of the time. Finally, to resolve the issue, I found some kiddy socks at the drugstore, some cute little pink things with elastic at the top—and they were a perfect size for a goose. Each day then, after the bandaging, I would slip a sock over the foot and secure it with surgical tape. From then on, the bandage stayed put. But Mr. Quack was ever full of new challenges and surprises.

About two weeks into his recuperation I walked out onto the porch one morning to find the straw had been reduced to a soggy matted swamp. Quack was there, proudly in the middle of his water bowl, enjoying his morning lustrations. He looked very pleased with himself. I had to laugh. After all, he was feeling well enough to want to bathe again.

After that, taking his cue, I scrambled around the garage and finally located an old metal tray which could serve as a kind of kiddy pool. It was a joy to see him in the mornings, waiting for the bath, ready to splash and clean his feathers which he did with great thoroughness and gusto. Naturally it made for some cleanup, but it didn't matter. He was a happy fellow, doing what geese like to do.

By then it was nearing the end of February, and throughout the month the wound had been healing well. Quack was ready to officially jettison his bandage for good. On our last visit to Dr. Dowdy, she asked when we were going to release him into the wild. The question came as something of a surprise. I hadn't thought about it. He was the one who came to us after all, and he wanted to stay. I was actually beginning to scope out locations in the yard for a goose house.

Lew and I looked at each other. "We're not sure," Lew shrugged.

"Well," said Dr. Dowdy, "if you do release him, I would wait till March. We'll be getting some nicer weather then, a little warmer. Might be better, you know?"

I thanked her profusely for taking on her strange patient, for getting us all through this experience, and I took out my checkbook and started to write. She immediately touched my hand.

"No. There's no charge. He's a wild animal. I was glad to help you."

"Please," I said, "let us pay you. You've done so much." But she was firm.

"If you would like to give a donation to some group that helps animals, that would be very nice."

"I certainly will," I said, and gave this dear lady a huge hug. She was truly a gentle Samaritan and I was merely a beneficiary in her eternal debt.

***

There was nothing to do now but wait for warmer weather, give Quack his normal care of food and water and clean straw. I spent some time on the porch stroking him, thinking about plans for the goose shelter. He showed no inclination toward leaving, and I mistakenly assumed that would always be the case. But I also didn't feel a complete sense of comfort with keeping him, for I wasn't really sure what was best for him. As it was, the decision was not mine to make.

It was in the first week of March. I hadn't slept well, and uncharacteristically arose one morning before daybreak, checking first, as I always did, on Quack. I discovered that he was up before me, leaving his nest of straw, and somehow surmounting the wooden fence of the pen. I found him unnaturally walking back and forth in the small space between the enclosure and the screens, seemingly in great agitation.

I went around and lifted him back into his pen, gave him some poultry pellets, and began to make breakfast for myself in the adjacent kitchen, but soon however, I heard a squawk and he was out again, this time pecking feverishly at a window.

"What's the matter with you?" I asked, as though I expected an answer, looking around for some explanation for this behavior. He didn't look my way or offer a clue, just resumed his fixation on the river flowing below the hill, quacking and calling out for something I had no language to discern. What did he want? Why was he so agitated?

I don't know what I was thinking then. I know that what I did wasn't something predetermined, any more than I could have predicted his behavior that morning. It was, however, the only thing that seemed right to do. I turned and opened the porch door, holding it ajar and looking back.

I take it that he must have felt the coolness of the air sliding in from outside, for he limped over and stood at my feet in the doorway, surveying as if for the first time this huge and white world outside.

It was perhaps a morning such as only comes in early March, when the snows have begun to slowly melt away and the sun has passed its nadir, riding higher in the northern sky. Across the river the first pale light rose from behind an arc of trees on the Sheepscot hills, traces of pink shimmering through the ice on the river banks. A winter quiet touched the valley and tiny cracklings of frost spoke brittlely in the trees. He hopped down the steps then and I knew that he was leaving.

He stood on the top of the snowy hill, looking east toward the sun, where he seemed touched by a new awareness. It was there that he began to call softly, cocking his head now and then as if waiting for some small echo to return back. I stood there with him, waiting in the snow.

It was a small fluttering at first, barely audible in the quiet morning—a far cry, a single echo from the expanse of the river below—and he answered back. Then a soft wave began rising, from all around on the icy shores, a chorus of many cries, lifting and growing stronger, rising in the morning air. It was a song from voice to voice, a cry of call to call, wafting up the hill and overwhelming the quiet dawn.

They were behind the island, his flock, and they knew his call. He began running then, running and raising his wings as the air came up the hill and carried him aloft with it. I watched as he floated in a beautiful glide far out over the river. When he drifted to the island I saw them join him there, and there followed a sound of such rejoicing that I doubt I will ever hear its like again.

I stood on the frozen hill, shivering in my slippers and housecoat, tears falling on the snow. He had determined the time of his leaving. It was not our decision to make.

***

It has been three years since he returned to his flock, and it was a good choice after all. I still see him everyday on the river. We have that, and I know he remembers me. He spends his time now with the one-eyed goose and another of strange coloration that I simply call Pinkie.

Sometimes I still wonder about his visit, wonder why he came up my field on that winter day, why he was so insistent on staying, and then, why he determined it was time to leave.

He never came up again.

He is out there now, small and probably old, still walking with a little limp. He has brought the others to me, and I feed them all in winter, and watch over them as best I can. We are bonded you see, he and I, allied in some strange alchemy of wings and feathers and drifting snow that brushed my leg as I stood on a hill once, feeding a flock of gulls. It's an alliance I did not choose, one as mysterious as any I've ever known. I have no answers for it, but I stopped looking for answers long ago, for, as my mother would say, well—that's just the way of it.

There is always one moment in childhood
when a door opens and lets the future in.
—Deepak Chopra

The Wreck of the *Esmerelda*

Not long ago, as I was cleaning out a little-used cupboard at our summer house, I came upon a crumpled piece of parchment. Although it looked to be ancient, it was only 12 years old, a tea-stained, burnt-edged document with notations in archaic English, written with a crowquill pen. How did it get there? Where did such an oddity come from? It was a map, a curious treasure map, and it led to the wreck of the *Esmerelda*.

I guess you would think that discovering a Spanish shipwreck, one nearly 300 years old, is a near impossible thing to do on the coast of Maine. Ordinarily, I would agree, but then you probably haven't visited Round Pond Harbor, or seen the old wreck fading there. The ship may be something of a mental reconstruction now, a few timbers and a chine board disintegrating amid rackstrewn rocks, yet she was once a great ship, one that held a vast repository of treasure and hope. And her story all began on a June day in the first summer we bought the Round Pond house.

***

Outside was a stunningly bright day, the harbor stretching below me like a shining gem as I tried to weed among the lupine and wildflowers in what might loosely be called our front yard. The phone rang and I hurried inside. It was Lew's sister, Pat. We had barely settled in, yet she wanted to come and visit us.

We adored Pat, a dear sister—and her visits were always welcome—but something in her voice was unusually tense and restrained. I wondered what was wrong. She said she was taking some time off work and would like to stay for ten days—if that was all right with us. And, yes, she would be glad to travel light because she knew we had much refurbishing to do and little storage space. The dogs and cat would stay in Pittsburgh in the care of a friend. And, yes, she was tired and looking forward to this visit greatly. Then, as we knew, she was briefly caring for two foster children and asked if she could bring them along.

Pat had previously described the girl as "11 and a little difficult"; the boy as "13, quiet, and with some emotional problems, particularly with anger management." That day she told us the children's mother, with a disastrous plethora of dependency problems, had recently passed away. Sadly, the only relative remaining was the mother's brother and he wanted nothing to do with raising two young children. As a last refuge, Pat said she had taken the children into temporary foster care in her home until more permanent arrangements could be found. Could she bring them?

"Of course," I said. "We would love to get to know the kids." The children were obviously going through a horrific upheaval and a trip to Maine might help to ease some of the pain of their loss ....and yet, when I told this to Lew, I would be less than truthful if I didn't say that he harbored a wee bit of trepidation, of concern about what we might be getting into.

That year it was a brutally hot summer, uncharacteristic for Maine, and they arrived from Pittsburgh, sweaty and rumpled a few days later. After the 14-hour drive, Pat was drained and immediately wilted on the front porch where a cool breeze was coming up from the harbor. She limply introduced us to Josh and Darla.

Josh made no eye contact. He mumbled a dispirited

hello, looking absently at his feet, the ultimate safe distractions of self-conscious adolescence. I thought he was thin and tall for 13, haggard-looking beyond his young years. Darla on the other hand was a cheery-faced rotund little girl who smiled broadly. She was wearing a cute denim outfit with suspenders criss-crossed over her tee shirt, something new Pat had bought her for the trip.

Both children stood awkwardly on the front porch, looking unsure of where to go or what to do. I brought out some iced tea which they accepted wordlessly and Pat and Lew talked for a few minutes about the difficulty of the trip. Then I asked the kids what they thought of Maine.

I knew that neither of them had ever taken a trip before, never even gone beyond the confines of their Pittsburgh suburb, yet that day, neither had the least bit of interest in looking at the bay and harbor that spread like radiant diamonds behind their heads.

I got only a shrug to my first query, so I tried again.

"Would you like to take a walk?" I asked, fishing for some form of activity. "Perhaps that would feel good after riding so long in a cramped car?"

"No, we're okay," Darla said, continuing to stand there, immobile.

"Well maybe you'd like to walk the dogs, look around in back and see the yard?"

"Uh-un. No, that's all right."

I kept trying. "How about your room? Maybe get settled in?"

"Okay..." came the unenthusiastic reply.

Pat, being mindful of our spare furnishings, had considerately purchased two cots and some bedding on her way through Brunswick, and she and Lew hauled them up the steep Victorian stairway and assembled the furniture in the kid's designated room—a peak-roofed bedroom with a dormer window overlooking the harbor, and an adjacent bath of 1940's vintage. I had cleaned the room the day before from a winter's worth of dust, cobwebs, and dead flies, then hung some sailing prints on the walls, (taking down my artwork after thinking about Josh's tendency toward violence, something Lew's mother had auspiciously warned us about.) I arranged some lobster buoys and bait bags filled with shells on the little chimney shelf that ran up the center of the room, then placed a small table in a corner with two chairs, a deck of cards, some games and a checkerboard, drawing paper and a few colored pens.

As Pat and I finished assembling the beds, Josh stood in the doorway, looking pale and distressed.

"W-Where's the TV?" he asked.

"We don't have one," I replied simply.

"N-not even d-downstairs?" he asked, his face now incredulous, as if he had landed among a tribe of Stone Age Neanderthals.

"No. Not even downstairs, not anywhere," I answered. "We don't really watch TV out here."

His eyes grew the size of sand dollars, staring at Pat with an exasperated expression. Then heaving a sigh of disgust, he fell on his cot, face pressed tightly against the wall.

Pat shook her shoulders and looked away. I went downstairs to check on dinner.

***

Standing in the kitchen, I dismally regarded the great hulk of the wood stove, an Atlantic that I called *The Queen Mary.* It had been converted to propane many years ago, and when a spark was lit it took a few seconds for the gas to hiss, sputter, and finally ignite in a retort equal to the percussion of a small grenade.

I watched it warily, holding a match under a burner, standing as far back as I could till the queen inhaled a premonitory breath of gas....then Ka-Foom! Flames gallantly leapt halfway up the sides of the black pot, a cast iron cauldron of home-made tomato sauce.

I leaned backward and adjusted the burner down, breathing more easily.

I hoped the first meal would go well.

There were no precedents for making culinary judgments about it, for I knew that Josh and Darla existed on pizza and sodas and whatever junk food they could obtain in their young lives. Their mother never cooked. Pizza was now one of the few foods they would willingly eat.

I also knew that over the short time Pat had Josh and Darla living with her, she had tried, rather valiantly, to expand their diet. Fruits were now mildly acceptable, hamburgers and fried foods okay, but nearly everything else was verboten, especially the despised and rarely glimpsed vegetable.

Consequently that night vegetables were not high on the menu. I was making a fork-friendly form of pizza called spaghetti. With salad and fruit, I thought the kids would have a balanced meal. If they would eat it.

That evening we sat down to a table set with lovely glasses, antique Willow Ware plates, cloth napkins, and a huge Ironstone pitcher of lupine centering the scene. I passed out plates of pasta and sauce, one by one, as Josh watched, surveying this communal grouping as if one from a visiting asteroid. He tepidly tasted the spaghetti, then threw caution to the winds and lunged happily in.

Darla, on the other hand, showed no such inclination and sat rigidly obstinate.

"I don't want this," she blurted.

"Try it," Pat said gently.

A hostile pause. "No. I'm not hungry."

Pat persisted. "Darla, you've had a long day and you need to eat something. Please try to eat."

"No."

We all sat motionless, waiting for what would come next.

Lew spoke then. "Darla, you can't walk to town and buy

snacks. There are no Burger Kings or Pizza Huts here. If you don't eat you are going to get very hungry."

This seemed to generate some sense of concern at the unavailability of viable food options, for Darla wrinkled her nose at the plate, as if trying to figure something out.

"What is it?" she asked, feigning ignorance, poking the noodles like a dead octopus with her fork.

"Oh come on, it's spaghetti," Lew said. "It has tomato sauce and meat on it, just like a pizza does." He was growing irritated.

"Yuck. It doesn't *sound* good," whined Darla, still glaring at the plate.

"Well," said Lew, now obviously annoyed, "that's why you eat with your *mouth* and not your *ears*."

Nobody got the joke.

It was, I thought, *going to be a long dinner.*

***

I can tell you that the first course was consumed in relative silence, except, of course, for Darla, whose minor grunts and moans punctuated the gathering. But I knew things were going to reach their difficult apex when I got up to get the salad—probably the *real* battleground of the meal.

I was in the kitchen, tossing salad, beside the queen, when I heard Lew's voice rising, the retired schoolteacher in him coming to the fore. When I returned, the only thing I heard was the sound of forks clicking on china plates.

"You know," Lew said, trying to make conversation, "we really want to make this a nice vacation for you, but we have just a few house rules. They may be different from what you're used to..."

He stopped and looked at the attentive little round face of Darla scrunched up in displeasure...

"But we will all have our meals together. We like to sit down and wait till everyone is at the table. Now, if you don't want to eat something, that's okay. We only ask that you try it. That's all. We only ask you to try things." Lew finished.

No response.

I tried to interject the old wedge technique of putting a positive spin on an unpalatable situation. "Look, you are on a vacation after all. You are in Maine, and when you go to a new place, that's what you do. You try new things!"

I was pleased when Josh reached over and speared a lettuce leaf. Darla reached for one with her fingers.

"Please remember to use your fork," Pat said very gently and encouragingly.

Darla complied without protest.

In this manner, we made it through our first meal.

***

It's pretty clear there isn't much to do in coastal Maine if you don't like walking, detest lobster, and hate saltwater. Such was the condition we found ourselves in those first two days. Josh seemed hermetically glued to his cot. He was in TV withdrawal and life had no raison d'etre. Darla had taken to a 24-hour argument with Pat which extended to everything from what clothes she was going to wear, to where they were going to go, to how long they were going to be there. She trekked to Pemaquid Beach but didn't like swimming because a threatening tuft of kelp lurked in the water. A kayak trip to see the island seals was a cacaphony of screams and complaints which scared the creatures away before anyone could get remotely close.

Yet with us, with me in particular, she was more malleable, or perhaps just more manipulative. But I knew in her conflicted and argumentative way that she was grieving, lost, and that she desperately wanted my approval.

As for Josh, he was displaying none of the anger we had worried about, but was profoundly quiet and withdrawn. He had never known a father, and Lew was trying mightily to engage him off his cot. You could say this became Lew's singular mission in life.

On the second day of the visit, he was able to get Josh off the bed, out of the house, down the hill to the dinghy dock, then into the dinghy for a row around the harbor. It was a masterful achievement. From the beginning, ever the teacher, he treated Josh like a fellow crewman and equal, instructing him in the basics of seamanship. Josh learned how to handle the oars, how to manage the etiquette and right-of-ways of other boaters, how to dock and secure the lines into proper seaman's knots. Surprisingly, the boy was a quick learner and Lew immediately trusted him to use the dinghy on his own—as long as he wore a life vest and didn't take the boat into the turbulent waters of Muscongus Bay.

After that, whenever Josh was tempted to slide back into TV torpor or other forms of lassitude, one of us would ask him to take us out in the dinghy. He always cheerfully complied, and we both praised him earnestly on his prowess at the oars. This seemed to change his demeanor greatly. He could now do what Mainers do, and he smiled more.

Darla, on the other hand, was a tougher nut to crack. Her contankerousness made it hard for her to concentrate for very long on any activity, and her anger seemed to find expression in any suggestion presented by Pat.

I used the small leverage I had with her and one afternoon took her to a craft shop in New Harbor where we bought some beads and shell ornaments. We spent a few hours afterwards stringing necklaces and anklets, chatting like girlfriends as we fashioned our jewelry on the front porch. We then had matching jewelry, a small connection. I also liked to walk with her down the hill to the Granite Hall Store. She always came back with penny candy and tiny ceramic animals. It was a start.

Of course, when she wasn't thus engaged, she was in a state of perpetual anger with Pat, only natural since poor Pat was the safest person to whom she could direct her rage. I worried about this conflict, wondered what to do to help, to ease the noisy argumentative drama that had invaded our peaceful little vacation home. Then one afternoon we went to Pemaquid Point.

***

I doubt there is a more magnificent natural fortress anywhere than the rocks of Pemaquid, striated and glacier-scoured spines of volcanic basalt that fall like giant steps to the sea. Josh and Darla skipped over the rocks like frisky seals, clearly enjoying themselves.

It was a gorgeous evening, waves crashing and blowing back sheer sheets of spume, tracings of orange light glazing the sea. We all sat on the great bluff facing east, and I told Josh—who had just seen *Titanic*—that it was this same North Atlantic water that had taken the famous ship down. His eyes grew intrigued, taken with what I presumed to be the embellished majesty of my tale. And I think it was then that the idea first formed. It was a vague thought at first, just a sense of possibility really...but one that reached out and eventually coalesced into a plan.

***

Ninety degrees. The week was impossible for Maine. Rarely do we have such heat— which is why no one has ever bothered with air-conditioning up here. Now, we desperately wished we had it.

Pat and Lew sought some cooling refuge in the gift shops, taking the kids to Wiscasset to look at boat models. I stayed home and gathered up some India ink and parchment paper and sat in front of a fan in my barn studio.

Sweat dripping off my nose, I tore the edges of a sheet of brown parchment paper till it looked exquisitely ragged. Then I took a lettering pen and drew a map. It was actually fairly easy to scribe, my Old English lettering book providing the guide.

Out in the harbor, at low tide, I knew there rested some old decaying ship's ribs, probably from a fishing boat beached there years ago. The wood was covered in mud and interspersed among rocks so that most people failed to notice the remains at all, but that day the planks morphed into the remnants of a great ship. They became the wreck of the *Esmerelda.*

In my engaging narrative, doubtless made deliriously more fanciful by the heat, one of the sailors of the *Esmerelda,* the sole survivor, had died and left a map. He had thrown his message in a bottle on the troubled seas, a clue to the gold of his lost ship. After a long and harrowing tale, the sailor signed his name with a flourish: *Ferdinand De La Mer.* I smiled to think of Ferdinand of the Sea.

Now the only thing left to do was to make a treasure and hide it in the prescribed locale. It should be easy—making the treasure. Except, I wondered, where do you find Spanish doubloons?

***

Gold coins. Doubloons. What about the doubloons? I had already disassembled necklaces of fake pearls, gaudy beads, rhinestones and glitter—and there was even one heavily beaded old medallion that had served duty as a Halloween costume piece years ago, one on which I had taped a peace symbol, presenting myself as an aging hippie. I had all the elements of a kingly trove, except the doubloons.

For the next two days, whenever we went out, I would sneak into gift shops and ask the same question, "Do you have any Spanish doubloons?"

They always surveyed me suspiciously, or hopelessly, till I told them what I wanted them for.

"Does anybody make anything like that?" I always asked.

“No,” was usually the answer, although I heard someone smirkingly titter as I left a shop in New Harbor, “Pity. She just missed Captain Kidd who took the last of our supply.”

I knew it probably was a fool’s errand, but after visiting most of the shops on the peninsula, the Granite Hall Store in Round Pond seemed the last fading outpost of possibility. They advertised that they carried everything, so why not try?

As I walked into the store, Sarah Herndon stood behind the counter patiently dispensing the usual penny candy to a handful of eager children. I searched quietly about the multitude of shelves, wandering from the first floor, to the second, then back again. Nothing. Finally, seeing I was empty-handed, Sarah queried, “Couldn’t find what you were looking for?”

“No, I guess not,” I said, discouraged...then hesitating because it sounded so ridiculous, “but you wouldn’t have any Spanish doubloons, would you?”

“Sure,” she said, not missing a beat, reaching under the counter and pulling out a bag of Spanish gold coins so perfect that I couldn’t believe they weren’t actually the real thing.

“We keep them all under the counter so the kids won’t see them. Sometimes people like to throw ‘em on the beach for the young ones to find. It’s fun for everyone, you know?”

Yes, I did know. I bought the whole bag. At three dollars and fifty cents, I considered it a bargain.

***

The Plot

“Do we have to eat lobster?” Darla whined as we sat at Shaw’s, overlooking the workboats and the watery bustle of tiny New Harbor.

“No, Darla,” I conceded. “You can get a hamburger tonight. Just try a piece of Josh’s lobster.”

I glanced at Josh happily munching away on his crustacean, thoroughly into Maine.

Darla disgustedly plucked a piece of claw. "Yuck" was the response.

"Okay," I said, "Get your burger."

We sat tightly together, opposite a red wharf, positioned in the actual salty eatery used the year before as a movie set for *Message in a Bottle.* Some locals in the restaurant had even made bit appearances in the film. We told the kids the plot of the film and they were spectacularly unmoved, yet somehow, despite the disinterest, I pursued my purpose and started to chum some bait...

"You know, bottles are often found on the coast." I stirred my lobster stew, reflectively drawing out the opening. "And some have notes...like in the movie...but once in awhile, one has a treasure map."

Darla paused in mid bite over her hamburger. Josh's lobster butter dribbled down his immobile chin.

"And pirates once prowled these waters, sailing up and down and pillaging."

"What's "pillashing"? asked Darla.

"*Pillaging.* It's when you take things," said Lew, frowning as Josh reached over and stole one of Darla's french fries.

"But the pirates here were said to bury their loot," Lew picked up the plotline then, "diamonds, coins, all kinds of treasure. Could be anywhere, any rocky beach."

Four small hands were now poised with food arrestingly suspended, eyes fully attentive.

"Aye, me hearties" quipped Lew in his best sneering guttural.

"You should be watchful," said Pat, "you might find your own bottle." She had been alerted to our gambit the night before and was fully engaged in it, almost too much so.

"W-were there lots of p-pirates right here? asked Josh. He still spoke little, and when he did he had a slight stutter.

"Sure, lots of 'em," embellished Lew, "the French, the

Spanish, the English—Bluebeard, Blackbeard, Kidd—more than I can name. Lots of wrecks on the coast. The thing is," said Lew, leaning in conspiratorially, "you two saw those rocks at Pemaquid the other day. You know how dangerous they could be. Shipwrecks are everywhere, but of course there wouldn't be much left of a wooden boat after hundreds of years, maybe just a few ribs or a plank here and there."

I thought the groundwork had been pretty well laid.

"Anyway—let's finish up," Lew said, "and we'll head home and stop at the salt pond so you two can walk the beach for awhile."

"Good," said Pat, "a postprandial promenade!" We all looked at her, bedazzled, or befuddled. She was always a voracious reader and a wordsmith, with a clever retort when least expected.

Laughing, I lifted my "postprandial" Bean bag, laden with towels and beach accessories, and felt the bottle roll in the bottom, the old wine bottle into which we had stuffed the map, then corked and appropriately sealed the contents with candle wax. We had fully hatched the plot and headed out to the salt pond.

The Rachel Carson Salt Pond is probably one of the most glorious and sparsely utilized beaches on the peninsula, a curved shoreline of beautifully rounded stones and glistening tidepools. That evening there were only three other people walking the rocky beach. Out in the blue water of Muscongus Bay the bare crowns of Haddock and Western Egg Island raised their heads above the sea, and farther out, the dappled cliffs of Monhegan caught the last rays of the western sun. The kids walked down to the pebbly beach and looked for starfish while I placed the green wine bottle, slightly askew, behind a little pile of rocks. We then called Darla and Josh to follow us up the beach.

I remember as we walked along that I purposely pointed back toward the lonely promontory where waves were spectacularly crashing...and it was then that Darla noticed the bottle. She immediately walked back, crouching down and lifting the green bottle up to the light. Maybe she didn't see anything inside for she made no particular comment. Josh however was soon there beside her and he noticed the parchment and had no such emotional containment. He screamed, "Th-there's s-some-th-thing in th-there, Darla! Oh, oh! Oh, what is it?"

This once retiring boy was jumping up and down, gesticulating, literally prancing, "Oh, oh!, Oh, oh!, you really f-f-found a bottle Darla! Oh y-you...y-you ...look, l-look, h-how old it l-looks...all th-that s-stuff on it!" (Lew had used a moldy wine bottle found in the garage, something to pass Spanish muster I presumed.)

"L-let's smash it!" screamed Josh, already reaching for a rock to complete the deed.

"No, no!" screamed Lew, grabbing his hand. "You should take it home and open it there. You don't want to get shattered glass on the beach—or damage the message inside!"

"Oh....r-r-r-right," Josh agreed, calming just barely, for he had suddenly discovered, it seemed, the joys of verbal communication.

"Oh, oh! Oh, oh! Look! Look! Darla, Darla, I c-can't believe you f-found that," he babbled all the way home.

***

That night even the dogs were attentive. As darkness enclosed us, huddled on the floor of our tiny living room, in the presence of candlelight the mystery of a 300-year-old shipwreck hovered in the gloom. We sat crosslegged, leaning toward the dim light, comrades in great ceremony amidst the smashed fragments of the bottle. Josh and Darla began to assemble the aged parchment, piece by torn piece, handling it like a fractured hieroglyphic papyrus found in the tomb of a pyramid.

Josh carefully laid out all the tatters on the rug, his amazement growing as he realized he was reconstructing a map.

"A map! Look, Darla! L-look at this! Look how old this is! L-look at this paper! How old could this be? What kind of map is it?" He had nearly stopped stuttering.

"Read the directions," Lew said. "What does it say?"

Abruptly the mood changed. Josh was crestfallen. We didn't know it but reading was his worst subject.

Darla volunteered to read it.

"No! No!" screamed Josh. "I-I w-want to do it. *You* f-found the bottle, Darla. *I* can do this."

He was quivering, shaking, but this was clearly his task and he was not about to relinquish it. His fingers moved painstakingly over the words, his mouth struggling to articulate the unfamiliar, archaic English. It was to be a long battle, one that raged in every portion of his body, from his hand, to his arm, and up to his trembling lips, forming and reforming the words silently. It was heartbreaking to see him in the candlelight, our little group gathered around him. He was struggling so, yet probably more motivated than he had ever been in his young life.

In the end, with a little help, he did it...and he paused and raised his face and looked about the room, amazed. Something fragile and significant passed there, in that moment, and I think we all felt it.

Pat quietly began to tape the map pieces together as Lew and I, Josh and Darla, sat silently on the floor, relishing the moment. We all knew, in our separate ways, that we were part of an adventure now. It was dark, only the distant light of the northern constellations coming through the long Victorian windows, but tomorrow, after breakfast, we would go, our hardy band, and seek the wreck of the *Esmerelda.*

***

You could say that for the adults, morning came much too early. The kids were noisily restless all night, then up before daybreak. It seemed that Josh, the eternal sleeper, had suddenly awakened from his long hibernation. When I arose and peeked in the room he was poring over the map, almost caressing it on the little corner table which now looked like a seaman's desk. Beside him were two compasses—something bought at the Granite Hall Store, no doubt at first light. This was true motivation.

Darla too was dressed and eager to go. I don't even remember if we ate breakfast. I only remember hauling down the street in the bleary-eyed dawn to Ulin's Beach with Darla holding the map and Josh checking compass readings, a new skill he seemed to have acquired through osmosis in his sleep.

"Pace 50 steps n-northwest, Darla, from the big rock...No, more to the r-right. Now turn due north and look for a d-dead tree," ordered Josh.

A withering look from Darla...no trees on this part of Ulin's Beach.

"Maybe there are some old roots in the bank," Lew said more than a little helpfully. "After all, it's been hundreds of years since Ferdinand made the map. Things have probably changed."

Darla looked. Still nothing.

Perhaps I had made a miscalculation on the map. I began to worry, but Lew saved the day.

"Well, Ferdinand was a man, and his feet were probably bigger than Darla's. Josh should try pacing the steps," said Lew.

(Now we were getting somewhere. Bigger strides. Closer to the treasure!)

As Josh paced, the always observant Darla skittered about the jutting rocks. As if on cue the tide was fortuitously falling and some feeble timbers were just beginning to make their presence known. The sharp-eyed Darla soon spied them.

"The *Esmerelda*!" she squealed, running straight into the

mud and dancing over the ribs like a lusty "pillasher."

"We're close, w-we're so close," stammered Josh. I could see the energy twitching through his body like sparks of neurological electricity.

Over the bank they both went then, scrambling among the dead roots, slipping about the rocks, slithering down mudbanks. Dirt flew from the rooty pits and crevasses. I'm not sure who first saw the corner of the wooden box. I only remember the cries that reverberated across the harbor, scaring the seagulls off their rocky perches.

The treasure of the *Esmerelda* had at last been found.

***

I have to admit it was all pretty authentic looking: the wooden box, the frayed cords of rope, the rusted metal latch, (no doubt from years buried in the muddy bank), and of course a princely treasure possibly entombed inside. What could Ferdinand have left behind?

The excitement was almost too much to contain in the small living room of the little cottage. We all gathered again, on the floor, with more candlelight, more suspense.

"Are we ready?" Darla finally asked, her hands visibly shaking. (Since she had found the bottle, she was designated as the official "opener.")

She reverently held the box on her lap, slowly removing the last rotting threads of rope. Cautiously she lifted the lid just a fraction, taking a quick glance through the slit, perhaps afraid of what she might find.

Gold coins immediately caught the taper's gleam, rhinestones picking up the prismed light, a silver medallion encrusted with glass rubies and emeralds glinting amongst the sparkling doubloons.

The box fell open and Darla stared aghast. Josh looked thunderstruck. Then, "We're rich," he said, the candlelight glowing on his face filled with the most exquisite awe. "Gold.

Gold...." he muttered as the coins tumbled like gleaming water droplets through his fingers.

The treasure was fondled over, piece by bejeweled piece, but the gold doubloons were the most astounding elements of all.

In the midst of this joy I quietly absented myself to the kitchen where I made a celebratory dessert. I didn't have much to work with, but I spread some layers of coconut, fruit, and instant pudding atop each other, then gave it some panache by serving it all in my fanciest glass goblets acquired for one dollar at a Round Pond yard sale.

It was a simple dessert, but as chefs say, "Presentation is everything."

When I came back into the living room with the glittering goblets, Josh asked, "What's this?"

"Oh, it's ambrosia," I replied, using as much import as I could summon, then added. "The Romans called it 'the nectar of the gods.' "

"Am-bro-si-a"...Josh mulled over the word without stuttering.

I could see that plain old fruit and pudding was being elevated to a princely status.

He was wearing the peace necklace of a king that night when he raised his spoon, toasting the occasion in perfect non-stammering pomp, "To ambrosia, nectar of the gods!"

***

There's a traditional saying, as old as it is true, hackneyed but full of warning: "Be careful what you wish for."

I had reason to consider this then, for the treasure was what we had wished for, and it had uplifted the spirits of two despondent children. It had given them reason to laugh together and to have an adventure. Especially for Josh, it had created a compelling reason for reading, for using a compass, and for following a map. For Darla, it had displaced some of her anger and given her the sense that she had a hawk-eyed knack for finding things, (as well as for wearing jewelry). Both children found an adventure in Maine. I was happy about this and wanted no more.

But the unfortunate downside was that the fantasy stoked a lot of false promises of wealth, even a kind of naive potential for greed. It became almost the be-all and end-all of the vacation, a particular source of fawning speculation on the part of Josh who seemed to see this cache as his passport to a life of ease.

It probably seems an innocent reaction now, maybe even a predictable one given the uncertain circumstances both children faced, but nevertheless, we fretted about the little lie we had created, wondered if we had done the right thing, if perhaps it had gone too far.

I tried to lay this concern aside for a few days and simply enjoy the remainder of our time together, which went exceedingly well.

Josh was proud of his boating skill and went rowing often. He was growing up and I felt he was just beginning to find some competency as a young man. Darla too was beginning to open up, would often walk to the Granite Hall Store with me, holding my hand, and I'd give her hugs and listen to her talk about her mother. Both children seemed to settle in, to adapt, and to cease their confrontations with Pat who always tried to be caring and supportive of them. And they ate whatever was put on the table. We never had a pizza in two weeks, and no one ever asked for it—nor did anyone lament the absence of a TV.

I guess however, it was inevitable as the end of the vacation approached that we had to tell the kids the truth about the treasure. Pat insisted on it, and I understood her reasoning. Still, I confess it was hard to destroy a fantasy that had provided such a wealth of joy. Lew and I delayed till the very last day.

I don't remember now exactly how we broached the subject. I only remember we told them that we loved them, that we loved having them with us, and that we had wanted them to have the fun of finding something special on the coast of Maine. We made the treasure map so they could know what other kids had found here—a bottle with a map, and an adventure.

It was Josh who seemed the most stricken. He was like a kid who's learned there's no Santa Claus. After he had suffered so much loss, I felt immediately terrible and blamed myself for cooking up the whole scheme. To salvage his pride, I suppose, he said he had noticed the faded image of the peace symbol on the necklace, and he had "wondered a little about that."

Darla, on the other hand, was totally unfazed. She said she'd had fun and didn't care. She was taking the jewelry home with her anyway!

So we sat again, all on the familiar floor in the familiar living room, looking at both of these children and feeling awful. I had no idea how to make any of this better.

Sometimes it seems that it is in moments of darkness that minor miracles can occur, and such, I believe, occurred that day...and it was Josh who made it happen. His boyish face suddenly seemed to be musing on something interesting, then widened into the birth of a grand idea.

"Let's rebury some of the treasure!" he proclaimed, "and I'll make a new map in a bottle. It will be something that someone else can find when they come here."

We all paused, considering his youthful and unbounded wisdom. And it was beautiful, really, a perfect circle. He had lived it, this dear boy, and wanted to pass it on.

So the next day Josh made a new map, duplicating the old one, and we reburied the treasure at Ulin's Beach. Darla sealed the map in a new bottle and Lew and Josh paddled out together to the entrance to Muscongus Bay where Josh launched the bottle into the water. Perhaps the outgoing tides would take it far. We could not know.

Pat and I walked down to the town dinghy dock to see them go.

"Thank you," she whispered softly.

"No, thank *you,*" I answered.

One could say it was the last act of a vacation, but it was not the end of a story. I happily relate that after Pat returned home, Josh and Darla were adopted by a kindly family. Josh knew a real father then, and he bloomed and did well in school. Darla loved her new family and eventually became a svelte and beautiful young girl. She was intelligent and I knew she would be fine. And somehow, through it all, I knew we had a small part in this, thanks to Pat, and to the *Esmerelda.*

***

I turn and place the torn parchment back in the little cupboard and close the warped wooden door. It will remain here for others to find and to wonder about...and I smile. Out in the harbor a few fading planks still remain, an old and wondrous repository of hope, unknown to all but us who lived the story.

Whenever I'm in Round Pond and I walk past the wreck now, I see it all again. I see two children, compasses in hand, scrambling over the jagged rocks. I see a boy with a map and a dream, trembling, as he reads directions to his garrulous little sister. I see them both again, dancing over the gnarled roots, peering into the crevices, slipping between the boulders, their footprints still lingering on some ageless shore.

I see them now secure in the knowledge that fantasy is not a superficiality, not an abstract or useless metaphor, but a joy essential to the human spirit, something as necessary as air, as light as hope. I saw this once, as a man and a boy, rowing a small boat, threw a message on the water.

I saw it in the wreck of the *Esmerelda.*

About the Author:

Belva Ann Prycel is a native of Millville, New Jersey, who grew up near the Delaware bayshores and Atlantic coast of which she so often writes. A graduate of Rowan College, an artist and former teacher, her paintings have been exhibited in museums, colleges, and galleries throughout the U.S. In 2001, she was one of four artists profiled in a New Jersey Network Public Television presentation, "Bayshore Artists: Celebrating Our Sense of Place."

Prycel has illustrated two books and was a frequent cover artist for South Jersey Magazine. Her writing has appeared in regional magazines, environmental journals, and two national anthologies.

In 2002, she moved to Sheepscot Village, Maine, with her husband Lewis and their dogs, Jolie and Tucker. Since that time, Prycel has written and illustrated three books of non-fiction, *Times and Tides*, *Water Tales*, and *Passage*, all memoirs of the coast and of her family. She currently enjoys painting, writing, living near water, and playing ragtime piano.

She may be contacted at baprycel@roadrunner.com.

www.ingramcontent.com/pod-product-compliance
Lightning Source LLC
Chambersburg PA
CBHW072147020426
42334CB00018B/1916
* 9 7 8 1 5 9 7 1 3 1 4 1 4 *